THE RANCHERS

THE RANCHERS

By the Editors of

TIME-LIFE BOOKS

with text by

Ogden Tanner

TIME-LIFE BOOKS / ALEXANDRIA, VIRGINIA

Time-Life Books Inc.
is a wholly owned subsidiary of

TIME INCORPORATED

Founder: Henry R. Luce 1898-1967

Editor-in-Chief: Henry Anatole Grunwald
President: J. Richard Munro
Chairman of the Board: Ralph P. Davidson
Corporate Editor: Jason McManus
Group Vice President, Books: Reginald K. Brack Jr.
Vice President, Books: George Artandi

TIME-LIFE BOOKS INC.

Editor: George Constable
Executive Editor: George Daniels
Editorial General Manager: Neal Goff
Director of Design: Louis Klein
Editorial Board: Dale M. Brown, Roberta Conlan,
Ellen Phillips, Gerry Schremp, Gerald Simons,
Rosalind Stubenberg, Kit van Tulleken, Henry Woodhead
Director of Research: Phyllis K. Wise
Director of Photography: John Conrad Weiser

President: William J. Henry
Senior Vice President: Christopher T. Linen
Vice Presidents: Stephen L. Bair, Robert A. Ellis,
John M. Fahey Jr., Juanita T. James, James L. Mercer,
Joanne A. Pello, Paul R. Stewart, Christian Strasser

THE OLD WEST

EDITORIAL STAFF FOR "THE RANCHERS"
Editor: Thomas H. Flaherty Jr.
Text Editors: Gregory Jaynes, John Manners
Designer: Edward Frank
Staff Writers: Dalton Delan, Margaret Fogarty,
Lee Hassig, David Johnson, Michael Roberts
Chief Researcher: Lois Gilman
Researchers: Karen M. Bates, Mary G. Burns,
Jane Coughran, Barbara Fleming, Jean Getlein, Pat Good,
Jane Jordan, Richard Kenin, Donna M. Lucey,
Carol Forsyth Mickey, Roger Warner
Copy Coordinator: Patricia Graber
Art Assistant: Lorraine D. Rivard
Picture Coordinator: Alex George
Editorial Assistant: Diane Bohrer
Special Contributors: Valerie Moolman, Russell Sackett,
David S. Thomson

EDITORIAL OPERATIONS
Design: Ellen Robling (assistant director)
Copy Room: Diane Ullius
Production: Celia Beattie
Quality Control: James J. Cox (director), Sally Collins
Library: Louise D. Forstall

THE AUTHOR: Ogden Tanner, a freelance writer with wide-ranging interests, has written numerous other volumes for TIME-LIFE BOOKS, including *The Canadians,* also in The Old West series; *The Battle of the Bulge,* in the World War II series; *Stress,* in the Human Behavior series; *New England Wilds* and *Urban Wilds,* in The American Wilderness series; and co-authored several books in The Encyclopedia of Gardening series. Previously he was a feature writer for the *San Francisco Chronicle,* associate editor of *House and Home* magazine, assistant managing editor of *Architectural Forum* and an editor with TIME-LIFE BOOKS.

THE COVER: Two cowboys, emerging from their lonely outpost on a huge Montana ranch, welcome a passing rider and invite him to share a meal with them. The scene was painted in 1904 by Charles M. Russell, himself a former cowboy. Russell, who saw Western ranching grow from a pioneering business into a colossal industry, knew that cowhands pulled "line duty" at least once a year and dreaded the task of roaming far and wide during the winter to collect strays and prevent them from freezing or starving to death. The frontispiece: This branding iron and others like it seared the famous Running W mark into the hides of hundreds of thousands of cattle, identifying them as the property of the immense King Ranch in deep-south Texas. The ranch's founder, Captain Richard King, designed the brand himself in the 1860s.

CORRESPONDENTS: Elisabeth Kraemer-Singh (Bonn); Margot Hapgood, Dorothy Bacon (London); Miriam Hsia, Susan Jonas, Lucy T. Voulgaris (New York); Maria Vincenza Aloisi, Josephine du Brusle (Paris); Ann Natanson (Rome). Valuable assistance was also provided by: Loral Steinbarth (Chicago); Emory J. Anderson (Jackson, Wyoming); Carolyn T. Chubet (New York); Ron White (San Antonio); Janet Zich (San Francisco).

Other Publications:

YOUR HOME
THE ENCHANTED WORLD
THE KODAK LIBRARY OF
  CREATIVE PHOTOGRAPHY
GREAT MEALS IN MINUTES
THE CIVIL WAR
PLANET EARTH
COLLECTOR'S LIBRARY OF THE
  CIVIL WAR
THE EPIC OF FLIGHT
THE GOOD COOK
THE SEAFARERS
WORLD WAR II
HOME REPAIR AND IMPROVEMENT

For information on and a full description
of any of the Time-Life Books series
listed above, please write:
Reader Information
Time-Life Books
541 North Fairbanks Court
Chicago, Illinois 60611

*This volume is one of a series that
chronicles the history of the American West
from the early 16th Century to the end of
the 19th Century.*

Time-Life Books.
  The ranchers / by the editors of Time-Life Books; with text by
Ogden Tanner. — Alexandria, Va.: Time-Life Books, c1977.
  240 p.:ill. (some col.); 29 cm. — (The Old West)
  Bibliography: p. 236-237.
  Includes index.
  SUMMARY: Describes in text and illustrations the development
of large ranches in the western plains, the impact of these
establishments on the economy of the area, their organization,
and some famous ranches and their owners.
  1. Ranch life — The West — History. 2. The West — History —
1848-1950. 3. Frontier and pioneer life — The West.
  1. Ranch life. 2. The West — History. 3. Frontier and
pioneer life
  I. Tanner, Ogden. II. Title. III. Series: The Old West
(New York)
F596.T52 1977   978'.02   77-85283
ISBN 0-8094-1510-0
ISBN 0-8094-1509-7 lib. bdg.
ISBN 0-8094-1508-9 ret. ed.

CONTENTS

Partners George Woodman and Arthur Huidekoper *(lower left)* survey their Deep Creek ranch in North Dakota around 1890.

1 | A life carved out of the Plains

They were "men who live in the open, who tend their herds on horseback, who go armed and ready to guard their lives by their own prowess, and who call no man master." Thus did Teddy Roosevelt describe the ranchers, a resolute breed who carved a great industry out of the Western wilderness.

The ranchers—women as well as men—found a land that brought out the most in them. They in turn made the most of the land, but not until they had learned to cope with solitude and failure, backbreaking labor and the hazards of grappling with nature and with each other.

Many ranchers were lone enterprisers; others represented absentee Eastern or European investors. Together they shared an independence that only open spaces can bring and a determination to build something lasting.

They bought land and cattle from the Mexicans in southeast Texas, then spread northward across the Great Plains to the Rocky Mountains and beyond. Some went away poorer than they arrived, but the survivors became barons of land and livestock who left an indelible brand on the Old West.

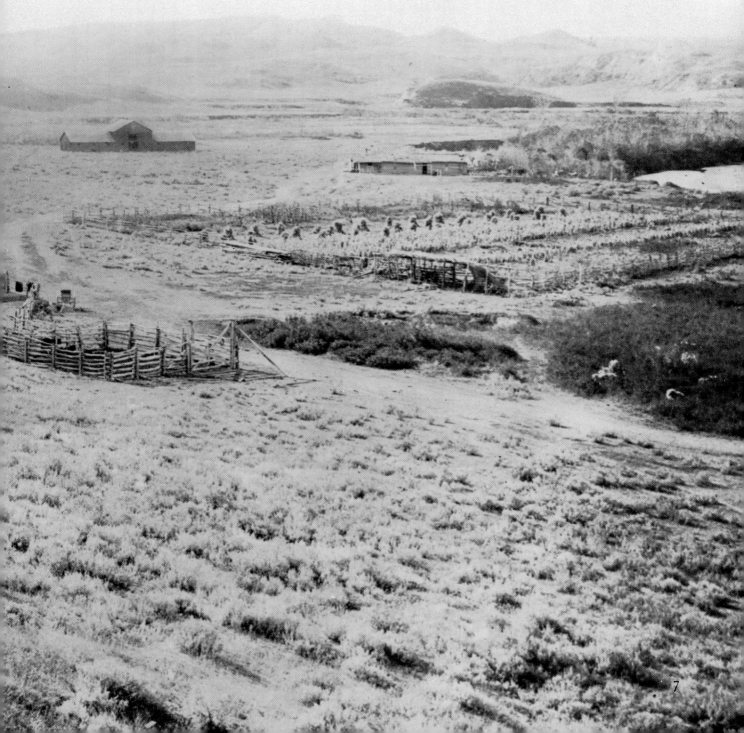

7

Andrew Drumm's 150,000-acre ranch at Cherokee Outlet was notorious in the 1880s as the worst place to work in Indian Territory, later Oklahoma. Drumm provided his men with tolerable housing but skimped on their meals and rousted them out for work long before the first cockcrow.

Midday dinner is a bountiful spread of home-grown beef and corn for the William Parmenter family of Colorado in 1889. But their faces betray the toil of providing it. Eating well was important, for the ranch workday began at sunup, continued until sundown and included chores for everyone.

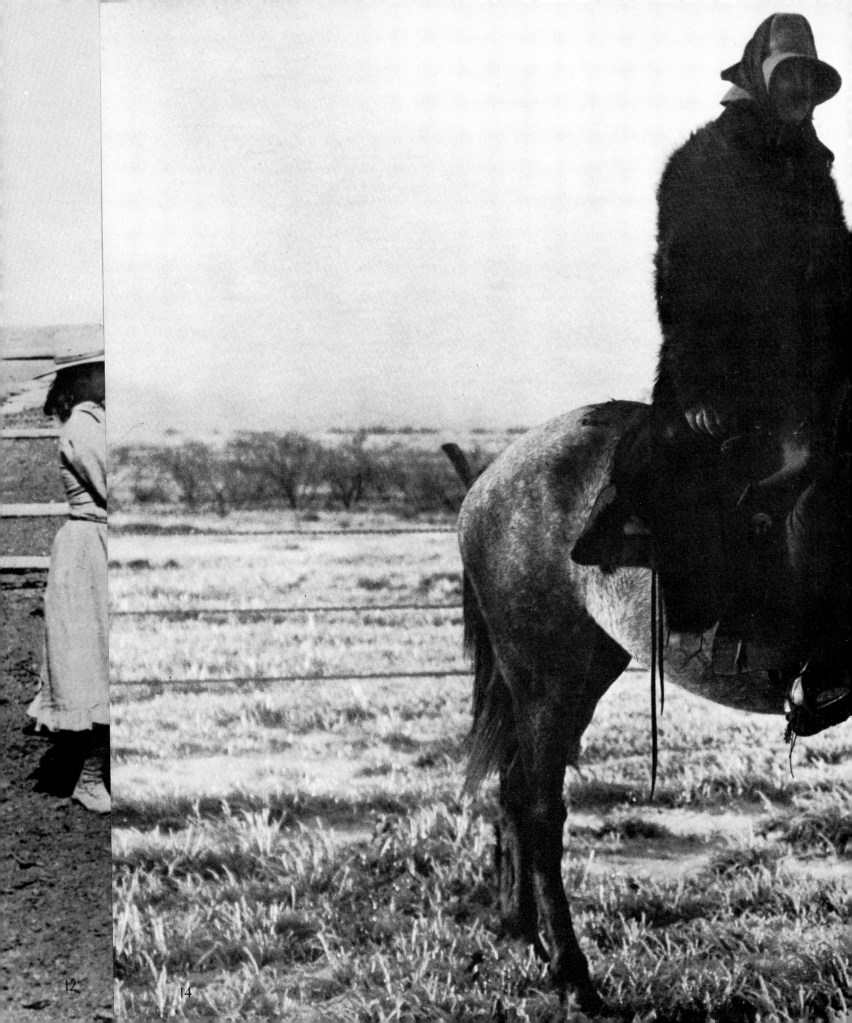

Bundled against the wind-driven snow of a "blue norther," Edwin Sanders patrols the barbed-wire border of his father's ranch in the Texas Panhandle at the turn of the century. Barbed wire, first used in 1874, let ranchers fence off grazing lands and inspired bitter feuds over boundaries.

His dark city hat sets off Scottish overseer Murdo Mackenzie *(center rear)* from the hired hands of the Matador Land and Cattle Company ranch in Texas in 1891. The Matador ranch was one of many owned by syndicates in Great Britain, which by the 1890s was importing more than 200,000 head of American cattle each year.

A pioneering generation of businessmen on horseback

The West was built by many hands, from trailblazing trappers and traders to prospectors who panned fortunes overnight and enterprisers who transported people and goods across rivers and rough terrain. But the real foundations of the West were laid by the men and women who became the first settlers throughout most of the enormous wilderness and who stuck it out and made the land produce new wealth every year, long after the gold and the fur-bearing animals were gone. They were the ranchers, a new breed of businessmen on horseback. Penetrating empty and inhospitable regions that had been shunned as wasteland, they raised livestock, using the West's abundant prairie grasses to produce the beef and mutton Americans ate, the leather and woolen goods Americans wore, and the horses Americans rode. In so doing, the ranchers made the West a paying proposition and thus opened it for sustained development by the settlers who followed them.

Besides the pioneer's expected ration of courage and determination, the rancher needed a trader's acumen, a speculator's eye for opportunity and a general's talent for action under fire. Some built up private baronies of land and livestock that gave them feudal powers at home and influence far beyond the borders of their domains. Others, no less heroic, scrabbled for bare survival against the will-bending isolation and relentless rigors of the hard land. Big and small, baron and bitter-ender, a generation of ranchers engraved their indelible brand on Western America. More than anyone else, they set its distinctive outlook, its dress, its vocabulary, its traditions and its style of living.

Starting in the Southwest, American cattle and sheep raisers spread their multiplying herds through the Great Plains, an immense and largely unclaimed land mass that had been avoided by settlers on the mistaken notion that it was too dry for growing crops. Defying Indians and outlaws—and sometimes common sense—they set up ranches on rolling plains and watered uplands from Texas to Montana and from Kansas to California. Nearly everywhere they went stock raising became the first lasting business.

In the heyday of Western ranching from 1866 to 1886, ranchers shipped more than 10 million cattle and one million sheep to market in the East. They created jobs for some 40,000 cowboys and herders, founded communities inhabited by half a million people and kept another million in the East and Midwest busy processing and transporting meat products.

Land was cheap or even free for the taking in the early days, and a number of cattlemen put together great ranches that covered several hundred thousand acres. In a few cases their holdings grew to a million acres or more. But survival for these giants, as well as for the many small ranchers who worked only a few thousand acres, was never easy. In many places ranchers were on their own for years and even decades before they could count on effective protection from soldiers, lawmen and the courts. During that period they had to defend themselves against not only Indians but also rustlers, squatters and one another. Then and afterward, they also had to cope with disasters beyond their control. There were winters of killing cold, summers of wasting drought, market prices that fluctuated unpredictably and financial panics in the East that undid years of perilous Western toil.

The biggest ranchers were usually the toughest and most resilient. Texan Richard King fought for several

Square-jawed Richard King (*seated*) and his partner Mifflin Kenedy, photographed in Brownsville during the 1850s, were both successful riverboat captains before they pioneered Texas cattle ranching.

Surveyors plan the expansion of Brownsville in the early 1850s. Located at the southernmost tip of Texas near the mouth of the Rio

years to hold his ranch against organized rustlers, suffering the loss of some 50,000 cattle. Another Texan, Charles Goodnight, fought the Comanches as a Texas Ranger and went broke at least twice before he put together a million-acre domain in an enormous canyon in the Panhandle. For sheer imagination and drive few men of any era equal Californian Henry Miller, an immigrant butcher boy who came West with six dollars in his pocket and built a ranching empire that spread over three states. At the peak of his career Miller controlled around 15 million acres.

Such men were far too ambitious to think of ranching as an end in itself. Using their cattle profits shrewdly, many of them acquired newspapers, banks, hotels, stores—and political power. Wyoming ranch-er Francis Warren invested in 30 different businesses and made enough friends to get himself elected to the U.S. Senate. John Chisum, a Tennessee-born Texan, moved his huge operation west to the Pecos River valley, where he ruled half of New Mexico without recourse to the ballot box. His authority was a small army of gun-slick cowboys.

In the 1870s the fabulous success of these cattle kings increasingly caught the eye of Eastern financiers. They saw in the booming, cash-hungry West a chance to increase their capital faster than they could in their heavily industrialized home states. They saw that Americans had recently developed a strong taste for beef, and they concluded that cattle prices, like the cow in the nursery rhyme, would surely jump over the

20

Grande, Brownsville enjoyed a lively river trade and was the headquarters for King, Kenedy & Company's fleet of small steamboats.

moon. In anticipating a brilliant future for Western ranching, they hastened its arrival.

Enormous sums of money flowed west from Wall Street banks and Chicago board rooms as capitalists scrambled to invest in beef on the hoof; Joseph Ames, a rich Yankee, summed it up: "You couldn't keep me out." As individuals and as corporations, Eastern investors grabbed up land, formed ever-greater ranches stocked with ever-larger herds and entrusted their operations to skilled Western managers like R. G. Head, who in the 1880s was paid the princely sum of $2,000 a month for running the far-flung ranching operations of the Prairie Cattle Company. In addition to the absentee landlords, many affluent Easterners and more than a few titled Europeans settled in the West and set up splendid ranches, sparing no expense to raise meatier cattle and faster horses.

But Western stock raising was changing radically even as it mushroomed. Barbed-wire fencing, introduced in the 1870s, began cutting up the open range. By then great bands of sheep were close-cropping the grasses of unoccupied prairie lands, leaving nothing but stubble for cattle herds too numerous to be supported on their owners' ranches. Still worse, hordes of belligerent farmers began encroaching on the range.

However, the cattlemen proved to be their own worst enemies. Aided by their enthusiastic Eastern backers, they had built up their business with an excess of optimism; their ranches became overextended, overstocked, overgrazed and mortgaged to a point far beyond their cash value. The results became painfully clear in the winter of 1886-1887, when the whole industry was badly shaken by murderously cold weather, followed by plummeting cattle prices as ranchers ruined by the winter kill rushed to sell out.

Stunned by widespread bankruptcies, ranchers finally moved to put their business on a sound footing. Then even the farmers proved useful—as buyers for surplus ranch land. The surviving ranchers concentrated on improved breeding and feeding techniques, producing more and better livestock on less and less acreage. Much to the sorrow of old veterans, ranching's pioneer years were drawing to a close. The excitement of that gaudy, slapdash, violent boom time lived on mainly in the imaginations of dude-ranch visitors and readers of romantic Western novels.

In planning realistically for changing times, many ranchers looked for guidance to the prime movers of their industry: the Texans. Western ranching started in Texas, and between 1866 and 1880 Texans alone had sent nearly five million cattle to market in the East. They had driven two million more—plus uncounted sheep and horses—into the Great Plains to stock the vast majority of new ranches there.

If any one ranch was a blueprint for success, it was the legendary King Ranch in deep-south Texas. One of the first and in the end the most durable of the great ranches, it continued to expand and prosper even through years when others diminished or disappeared. It became the world's largest stock-raising operation and the only American ranch to develop a new breed of beef cattle, the cherry-red Santa Gertrudis.

The King Ranch's founder, Richard King, was a bold trailblazer yet as sound as a Boston banker. He dared to start raising stock back in 1852, when the whole trans-Mississippi West had fewer than 600,000 potential customers. King encountered all of the problems that had plagued ranchers since the Spanish conquistadors first imported cattle, horses and sheep in the 16th Century. But he adapted useful Spanish techniques, introduced new ones that became standard throughout the West and built up his ranch with patience and care. The place he chose to do all this came to be recognized as the birthplace and breeding ground of American ranching: the broad belt of embattled prairie land between the Rio Grande and the Nueces rivers.

In 1852 Captain Richard King was a partner in a riverboat company that ferried goods up and down the Rio Grande from Brownsville, the southernmost town in Texas. Any other man would have been content: at 27 King had come far, the hard way. The son of poor Irish immigrants, he had run away from their New York City slum as a boy of 11, stowing away aboard a ship bound for the Gulf of Mexico. That journey committed him to a rough-and-tumble career in Southern waters and on Texas docks.

Over the next 11 years King worked his way up in the steamer business; he studied the arithmetic of freight and trade, earned his pilot's license and the title of captain, and carried troops and supplies on the Rio Grande when the Mexican War broke out in 1846. Later he went into business with a wartime friend, Mifflin Kenedy, and began building up a riverboat fleet that would number 22 vessels by 1865. But King was restless. His modest savings were burning a hole in his pocket. He was ready to take a stab at some risky business—a sideline that might make him a major capitalist before he turned gray.

King had another reason for his discontent: he was still a rootless bachelor. Never having enjoyed home or family, he wanted both more than most men. There was a proper, pretty, cultured woman who interested King: Henrietta Chamberlain, the 17-year-old daughter of a Presbyterian minister. King had met her in 1850, just after she arrived with her father in Brownsville. The Chamberlains were living temporarily in a houseboat that happened to be blocking King's slip when he returned from a trip downriver to the Gulf of Mexico. King cursed up a storm, and Henrietta scolded him for his blue language and bad manners. He liked her spirit and after a few meetings decided he would marry her as soon as possible.

One look at King suggested that he would get Henrietta—and anything else he went after. He stood nearly six feet tall, was broad-shouldered, heavily muscled and boldly good-looking, with a big determined jaw and fierce blue eyes. On his way up he had fought with his fists as well as his nimble mind, and he enjoyed both kinds of contests. A friend later reported that the captain kept a big Irish brawler on his payroll

Henrietta King, wife of the millionaire rancher, never forgot the stern Protestant teachings she had learned as a girl *(left)*. Eschewing displays of wealth, she refused to wear King's gift of diamond earrings until she had them covered with enamel.

The King ranch house grew from a frame building *(above)* to a two-story structure with an annex boasting 10 bedrooms *(left)*. In 1912 it was destroyed by a fire probably started by a disgruntled gardener.

mainly to fight with him when he wanted to let off steam. Another friend said of King, "I never knew a rougher man, nor a better man." This was not a man who would suffer frustration quietly or for long.

Small wonder, then, that King was responsive when he learned that the town of Corpus Christi was promoting a fair to attract settlers and businesses to the area. On a warm April day in 1852, King mounted up—awkwardly, since he rode very little—and headed north with a few friends for Corpus Christi, about 170 miles from Brownsville.

They traveled through sunny prairies that had seen the first marches of the Mexican War and that had been used before and after as a thoroughfare by northward-raiding Mexican bandits and by southward-raiding Comanches, Apaches and sundry Texas outlaws. Spanish grandees had fought valiantly, but with little success, to make ranching pay here, and their Mexican successors had finally abandoned the region in the 1830s in the face of increasing violence. The Mexicans called it *El Desierto de los Muertos*—The Desert of the Dead. South of the Nueces River valley the land was virtually uninhabited except for mustang herds, the spirited descendants of domesticated horses left by Mexican ranchers returning to their homeland in defeat. From those mustangs came the American name for the region: the Wild Horse Desert.

King and earlier travelers were astonished by the size of the mustang herds. During the 1846 American invasion of Mexico, a young Army lieutenant named Ulysses S. Grant saw herds so large that he doubted "that they all could have been corraled in the State of Rhode Island, or Delaware, at one time." A number of poor Texans had started ranching north of the Nueces by capturing and breaking the wild horses, then using them to round up a herd of similarly abandoned, free-roaming cattle. One such rancher, Thomas Dwyer, wrote of "thousands and tens of thousands of wild horses running in immense herds as far as the eye or telescope could sweep the horizon. The whole country seemed to be running!"

As King rode on he realized that the Wild Horse Desert had much more to offer than free horses. About 125 miles north of Brownsville, the captain and his friends noted that the desert vegetation was getting greener, and they paused to drink the clear, cool waters of a tree-shaded stream known as Santa Gertrudis Creek. King gazed beyond the grove of live oaks and anaqua trees and saw the prairie rolling away to the horizon, its grasses rich and waist high and splashed with red, gold and blue wild flowers. Among the patches of mesquite trees and tall prickly-pear cactus, game of all sorts abounded: antelope, deer, wild turkey, quail. King had probably first heard of the Santa Gertrudis area from a friend and popular local hero, Texas Ranger and militiaman Gideon Lewis. Better known as "Legs" for his tireless marching during the Mexican hostilities, Lewis considered the area a rancher's paradise, and King could see why.

The captain and his companions reached Corpus Christi without a discouraging word. While strolling among the exhibits at the fair, King ran into Legs Lewis, and the encounter led to much more than either man expected. Lewis took time off from his favorite avocation, womanizing, to discuss with King the possibilities of ranching in the Santa Gertrudis area. A plan evolved for a curious partnership. King would finance and set up a cattle camp on Santa Gertrudis Creek, and Lewis, while leading his militia patrols, would guard and supervise the fledgling ranch, allowing King to continue his profitable riverboating.

King had no illusions about the business he was getting into; he quickly found out enough about Texas ranching (as distinct from raising dairy cattle) to know that it was about as chancy as playing poker with riverboat gamblers. It was actually only half a business. Texas longhorns, the captured descendants of abandoned Mexican cattle, were being raised mainly for their hides and fat, which was rendered to make soap and tallow candles; in these prerefrigeration years most of the meat was unmarketable—it was sold locally for a few cents a pound. Beef could not be preserved long enough to ship to distant population centers, and transporting live animals to market by boat was unfeasible. This was the central problem that had frustrated Spanish and Mexican ranchers, and it was still frustrating the Texas stock raisers north of the Nueces River and around San Antonio.

It was true, King learned, that beef on the hoof could be herded overland to distant markets to be butchered there. Texas longhorns had withstood drives to New Orleans, to Chicago and even, just to prove it could be done, to New York City. After the 1849 gold rush to California, several Texas ranchers had made a profit by trailing longhorns all the way to the West Coast, selling them at up to $100 a head to feed the hordes of prospectors. But even under the best circumstances, with no Indian or outlaw raids and with only normal cattle losses along the way, trail drives of more than 1,000 miles were a shaky way of doing business on a regular basis. In the time it took a herd to reach market, falling cattle prices could—and often did—make the trip unprofitable.

Yet the statistics were irresistible. A mature, market-ready longhorn that was valued in Texas at three dollars a head might bring $30 at any cattle market. Cattle being fecund, a herd normally doubled in size in three years. The animals grazed on free or cheap land, and up to 1,000 head could be tended by a single cowboy who earned perhaps $25 a month. Thus enormous profits could be made at ranching—but not until the three-dollar steer could be delivered to the $30 market swiftly, cheaply and reliably.

The obvious solution, even then being discussed by cattlemen, financiers and politicians, was a transcontinental railroad. Though the railroad would not come for another 15 years, King plunged into ranching with impatient optimism, yet with unhurried thoroughness. He could simply have occupied and used the vacant Santa Gertrudis land; many honest men elsewhere were doing the same thing (and would pay dearly for their informality in interminable lawsuits once the property was improved and valuable). But King searched for and found the Mendiola family, heir to the original Spanish land grant. The Mendiolas, who had left the land a generation before and had no plans to return, gladly agreed to sell their 15,500 acres for $300. They set their hands and seals to a warranty deed in July 1853.

All the time that King could spare from his riverboat business he now spent at the Santa Gertrudis ranch. He even made a special trip up from Brownsville to serve as a chain carrier for the surveyor he hired to confirm the vague boundaries of the Spanish land grant. All the money King could squeeze from his share in the riverboat company he plowed into the ranch. He soon bought, in his name and Lewis', a much larger adjacent property to the west, paying

$1,800 for 53,000 acres of prime grassland. The construction of ranch buildings went slowly. On a green rise of land near springs that fed Santa Gertrudis Creek, the partners first built primitive quarters and a corral made out of mesquite logs. Then, with the help of a few hired hands, they raised a cluster of earth-brown wattled huts and, to defend their rude camp, built a stockade and blockhouse that boasted a brass cannon. King would fight, if he must, to hold his lovely bloodstained prairie.

To ready the ranch for livestock, King and Lewis set their men to work building a rough dirt dam to trap water from a stream near their headquarters. By 1854 when a long drought gripped Mexican ranches across the Rio Grande, the Santa Gertrudis had plenty of stored water and the captain was able to buy thirsty, bony Mexican livestock at depressed prices. In the border towns of Mier and Camargo, he bought up animals of all sorts—not just cattle but also sheep, goats and horses. King was only being practical in deciding to spend money for horses instead of capturing wild mustangs free of cost. He needed tractable mounts at once and could not afford the long hard work of breaking and training the defiant mustangs.

The captain also looked to Mexico for ranch workers and skilled riders to tend his cattle herd and horse corral. King offered *vaqueros* 25 pesos a month plus board and keep—equal to the minimum of $25 a month paid to American cowboys.

And King offered fringe benefits—a tactic that would not occur to many Western ranchers for years. His master plan for staffing his ranch evolved during a purchasing trip south of the border. At a drought-stricken village below Camargo, he bought all the livestock available. Then, realizing that the villagers were left without a business to sustain them, he made them an offer: if they would come to work on the Santa Gertrudis, they could build homes of their own. The villagers recognized this arrangement, which resembled the feudal form Mexican ranching had taken since the days of the Spanish conquistadors. Having no better alternative, they agreed to King's offer and accepted him as their *patrón,* or protector.

More than 100 villagers—men, women and children—pulled up stakes and started north. They traveled in a long, noisy caravan, riding rickety two-wheeled *carretas,* pushing wheelbarrows full of clothes and household goods. On reaching the Santa Gertrudis the villagers soon learned that King was firm and demanding but—unlike the typical *patrones* they knew earlier—always fair and even kindly, taking a personal interest in their well-being. They gave him their unqualified loyalty and became the nucleus of *Los Kineños*—the King People, as the ranch workers and their families came to be called. They, their children and their children's children would live and work on the King Ranch, secure and respected as productive members of a self-sufficient society.

News of King's ambitious operations aroused lively curiosity to the north and south. Once or twice Mexican outlaws tested the ranch's defenses, but *Los Kineños* were handy with rifles and drove off the raiders; soon the Santa Gertrudis was left alone, except for minor rustling and an occasional sniper. In turn, the newfound peace along Santa Gertrudis Creek interested prospective ranchers. Encouraged by King's strong stand, Texans began moving south, claiming land and starting other ranches in the Wild Horse Desert. They regarded King as their leader.

Two events in the mid-1850s ended the formative stage of King's ranching business. One was a shocker that deprived King of his debonair partner. Legs Lewis was shot to death in Corpus Christi by the irate husband of his latest paramour. Lewis' death saddened King, but it enabled him to strengthen the business structure of the ranch. Legs had had little money to invest; he had contributed protection and shrewd advice. Now King incorporated the Santa Gertrudis under the name R. King and Company and got two new partners with sizeable capital to put into it. One was King's partner in the riverboat company, Mifflin Kenedy; the other was James Walworth, a steamboat captain who would be a silent partner.

The second milestone was a happy one. With the ranch solidly established, Richard King had a permanent home—though not yet a castle—to offer Henrietta Chamberlain, and the time had come to marry her. It had been no easy task to win her father's approval. King had had to court her formally, dress up like a gentleman, take constant pains to utter no sailor's oaths and even attend prayer meetings. But he got what he sought. On December 10, 1854, after the

Skillful *vaqueros* drive a herd of longhorns in a trail scene painted in the 1870s. Mexican riders for King and other Texas ranchers were

zealous guardians of their employers' cattle, and some *vaqueros* even went hungry during trail drives rather than butcher a single steer.

evening service at the Reverend Hiram Chamberlain's First Presbyterian Church in Brownsville, King left his seat and Henrietta left her usual place in the choir, and her father pronounced them husband and wife before the whole congregation.

King took his bride to the Santa Gertrudis in a stagecoach he had bought for the occasion. As they neared the ranch, grinning *vaqueros* rode out to greet the new Mrs. King—*La Patrona*. Henrietta was happy with her home, and she wrote, "I doubt if it falls to the lot of any bride to have had so happy a honeymoon. On horseback we roamed the broad prairies. When I grew tired my husband would spread a Mexican blanket for me and then I would take my siesta under the shade of the mesquite tree."

For the next five or six years everything on the Santa Gertrudis grew. The King family grew; daughter Henrietta, nicknamed Nettie, was born in 1856, daughter Ella in 1858, son Richard II in 1860. More Mexicans joined *Los Kineños,* and their families grew as well. Mrs. King took personal charge of them, supplying the needy and nursing the sick, and though she, like King, was a stern taskmaster, the ranch people came to adore *La Patrona.* And to accommodate the growing King and *Los Kineños* families, the ranch quarters grew.

King planned a new and much bigger ranch compound for his headquarters. He discussed the choice of sites with his enlarging circle of friends, many of whom the Kings entertained at both the Santa Gertrudis ranch and the Brownsville townhouse they bought next door to Mifflin Kenedy's. Among the new friends was Lieutenant Colonel Robert E. Lee, whom King met while shipping supplies to Army posts along the Rio Grande. Colonel Lee, an Army engineer and Virginia plantation owner experienced in land management, helped King choose the site for the ranch house on a height of ground not far from the crowded original headquarters. Reportedly, Lee also gave King a bit of advice: "Buy land; and never sell." Whether the precept came from Lee, King made it his motto, and his prairie-land properties continued to grow even as his new ranch house rose.

The permanent headquarters was completed by 1859, and the Kings moved into a rambling frame house with shaded galleries. It was connected by an open walkway to a building containing the kitchen and dining room, which King separated from the main house to minimize the fire hazard. Nearby stood a stone-walled commissary, bunkhouse and a lofty watchtower; scattered beyond were corrals, stables, wagon sheds, a blacksmith's shop and the houses of *Los Kineños*. Before long a one-room schoolhouse was built for the ranch hands' children, who did their lessons under the watchful eye of *La Patrona*.

With Mrs. King in full charge of daily routine, the captain was free to pursue stock raising and ranch business in the time he could spare away from the riverboat company. He bought more and more livestock, and the new purchases, together with his herds' increasing progeny, raised the assets of R. King and Company to 20,000 head of cattle and 3,000 horses by 1861.

In these growing years King did very little selling. In 1854 and 1855 the largest transactions recorded in his ledger were "mules and horses, $223" and "$1,000 worth of mares." But the horses King sold and the cattle he slaughtered for hide-and-tallow income were disposed of primarily to weed out inferior animals so that he could upgrade his breeding stock. The captain himself supervised roundups and indicated which animals were to go and which were to stay.

The cattle King bought and raised were predominantly longhorns, long-legged and durable, ideally suited—by their Spanish heritage and long naturalization—to the semiarid prairie lands of Texas and the rough terrain common elsewhere in the West. But the longhorn, a hardy, nimble beast that needed little water, produced less meat than the low-slung Eastern breeds of English origin. On the other hand, the Eastern cattle had trouble traveling on rugged ground and were more vulnerable to drought, disease, insects and heat. In order to combine the longhorn's durability with the meatiness of Eastern breeds, King began importing blooded Durhams to cross with his best native stock. Slowly his breeding experiments improved the quality of his herd. Texans who lacked the funds or foresight to use such a systematic breeding program were in for serious disappointments. In later years cattle dealers would pay about 20 per cent less for a Texas longhorn than for a Western crossbreed,

Camp Las Moras' C.S.A. near Fort Clark Texas March 1861.

and they would pay that with increasing reluctance.

Because the sale of cattle for beef was growing only slowly, King concentrated his attention on his horse herd; he later said of his ranch, "Horses made this a success." The captain bought and raised horses for ranch use and for sale as saddle, pack and harness animals. Horses were smarter and quicker on the hoof than cattle, and therefore easier to round up and to control on trail drives. They brought higher prices and were in demand by the many new ranchers and by the Army posts that were appearing throughout the West to protect settlers. Besides, horses had belatedly become King's pride and joy, and he bred them experimentally with all the fervor of an explorer.

King started his equine breeding program with advantages that many other ranchers in Texas did not share. Thanks to his riverboat company income, he was able to assemble a herd of sound Mexican ranch horses. These mounts were bigger, better-looking and more reliable than their throwback cousins in the Wild Horse Desert, which poor ranchers were obliged to capture and use. King crossbred his Mexican horses to upgrade his herd in general, improving the stamina, nimbleness and intelligence of his stock. But he also bred horses for a specific function that was essential to cattle ranching: for a cowboy to rope a runaway steer, he needed a mount that would start explosively, reach a full run in a few strides and maintain blazing speed for about a quarter mile. In breeding for these traits, King and other Texas ranchers gave rise to the Western quarter horse, which combined the best features of the rugged Spanish-descended horse and the fragile, high-strung English racing horse. In time the King Ranch would become a leader in

31

The Kings had their own capacious stagecoach to transport them between the Santa Gertrudis ranch and the towns of Brownsville and Corpus Christi, where they maintained houses and carried on extensive business. A team of four horses drew the coach, and armed outriders protected it from Indian and bandit attacks on the trail.

Captain King's 15-inch-high leather hatbox accompanied him on his frequent stagecoach trips. Its square shape and metal lock suggest that it may also have served as a case for carrying valuables, including cash and private papers.

the breeding of quarter horses.

King looked to the East for horses with English blood. He began buying well-bred Kentucky stallions and crossing them with Spanish mares in closely observed combinations. Cost was no object if King liked an animal's size, conformation or other qualities. He paid $600 for one stallion, a whacking high price in those days.

By 1861 King's zealous work and heavy investment had developed his stock to a point where he could afford to sell good animals, not just dispose of culls. Having high-quality stock, the captain had more customers than he could accommodate among his expanding number of neighbors in the Wild Horse Desert and to the north of the Nueces—in spite of the fact that Texas by now was bursting with cattle. Indeed, ranching in the Lone-Star State was caught up in a cycle of self-sustaining growth. Texas ranchers were selling more hides to Eastern leather-goods manufacturers and supplying more cattle for beef to Army posts, which now had to feed not only themselves but also whatever Indians the U.S. Cavalry had defeated and consigned to reservations. The growing markets encouraged veteran ranchers to raise bigger herds and attracted newcomers to the stock-raising business. Their search for new or larger grazing lands pushed the cattle frontier north and west into Texas plains where vanquished Indians had recently hunted the dwindling buffalo.

In sum, Texas ranchers in 1861 were ready for bigger things. If the railroad had come West right then, the cattle boom would have started about five years before it actually did. Instead, the Civil War came and plunged Texas ranchers—and everyone else—into five years of chaos.

Of Texas' 600,000-odd inhabitants, some 60,000 marched off to fight for the Confederacy, and 27,000 more were assigned to defend the state. Many ranch-

ers lost most of their cowboys. Then, while the northern ranches were very shorthanded, bands of Comanche horsemen made a violent comeback and drove the frontier southward by as much as 100 miles.

In the South, meanwhile, Richard King and a few other ranchers whose riders were predominantly Mexican had kept their crews almost intact. But with the outbreak of war, these ranchers lost their Eastern hide-and-tallow business and their sustaining horse trade with the Western posts of the U.S. Cavalry. They sold beef and mounts to the Confederate forces, but not nearly enough to make up the difference. Yet, in spite of the dismal business prospects, Richard King proceeded to make his first fortune.

The transplanted New Yorker, 36 when the war began, was a fiery Rebel, and he served with gallantry on the front where he was needed most—at home. When the Union Navy closed the South's ports with a bristling blockade, the Rio Grande became the lifeline of the Confederacy. King and Kenedy's steamboat company played a major role in the vital—and lucrative—work of ferrying the South's principal product, cotton, across the river to the Mexican town of Matamoros and bringing back British guns and ammunition that had been hauled overland from Mexican Gulf Coast ports. The ranch of R. King and Company became a depot and clearinghouse for millions of dollars worth of southbound cotton and northbound armaments, supplies and livestock.

King was a vigorous and imaginative agent. When Union forces began making forays up the Rio Grande, he put his steamers under Mexican registry, ran up Mexican flags and brazenly continued his traffic. King was provident—or perhaps prophetic. When Southern officers paid for his livestock or his international smuggling, the captain requested gold instead of Confederate greenbacks. King was also opportunistic enough to make huge profits by speculating in cotton.

And King was fast on his feet; a man marked for death by the Union Army had to be.

One of the times he took flight came in late December, 1863. A Yankee landing party had seized Brownsville and sent some cavalry north to the Santa Gertrudis to terminate the subversive career of the notorious Captain King. King, forewarned by a friend, left home at a gallop, confident the bluecoats would not bother a ranch full of non-combatants, including his wife, who was pregnant with their fifth child. He was wrong.

On their arrival, the Yankees started peppering the ranch house, and when an unarmed worker tried to inform them that the captain was not there, they shot him dead. Then, enraged by King's escape, they rode their horses through the house, smashing windows and furniture, collecting clothing and valuables. The raiders held the Santa Gertrudis for two days, keeping the ranch hands locked up while they loaded their booty on wagons and rounded up horses to take as prizes of war. Finally, on Christmas Eve they were alarmed by the reported approach of unidentified horsemen and headed south, leaving behind a real treasure—uncounted bales of cotton.

The next day was a grim Christmas at the Santa Gertrudis. Henrietta King, ashen but unharmed, was helped into a coach with her children and hurried off to the safety of friends north of the Nueces River. There, in February 1864, she gave birth to a son and defiantly named him Robert E. Lee King.

With his family out of the combat zone, Richard King pursued his daring duty to the war's end. He even served briefly with a home-guard troop. But the Confederacy died in 1865, and in the first gloomy light of peace, Texas ranchers saw that they had a strange disaster of abundance on their hands.

Texas was fairly drowning in cattle—about six million of them. Several generations of cattle had been born since the outbreak of war and, with most of the cowboys off fighting Yankees, thousands of young bulls that would have been castrated in normal times had bred at a fearful rate. To make matters worse, tens of thousands of cattle had wandered off their untended home ranges; then, in the last winter of the war a terrible cold wave had driven them south to intermingle with the herds in warmer climes.

During this so-called Big Drift, inestimable numbers of unbranded cattle milled around, free to anyone who cared to take them. But until markets were re-established, ranchers who had control of their herds could hardly afford to keep them much less acquire more. One stock dealer observed, "A man's poverty was estimated by the number of cattle he possessed."

It took most Texas ranchers a year to put their operations back into prewar order. Some herds—including one from Richard King's ranch—were driven to market in Missouri soon after the peace, and these Texas cattle became one of the first business ties to bind together the re-United States. But the Texas cattle business had barely been reorganized when it was totally revolutionized in 1867 by the long-awaited coming of the railroad.

That year, the Union Pacific, which in 1869 would become the first line to cross the continent, headed out from the vicinity of Omaha, Nebraska, into the midsection of the Great Plains. The advancing tracks immediately made stock raising feasible and alluring throughout hundreds of miles of nearly empty grasslands on either side of the right of way. Better still for the Texans, a second line—soon to be known as the Atchison, Topeka and Santa Fe—swung south from St. Louis in 1868 and passed through a succession of prairie hamlets in southern Kansas. These ramshackle way-stops—most notably Abilene and Dodge City—immediately became trail's-end cattle towns for immense cattle drives, and raucous

35

marketplaces for throngs of ranchers, cowboys and cattle buyers, not to mention cardsharps, prostitutes and gunfighters. The movement of Texas cattle to Kansas railheads increased by leaps and bounds; in 1871 no fewer than 700,000 longhorns were sold in Abilene alone. The Western cattle boom was on.

A few months before Abilene blossomed as the first Kansas market for eastbound beef, Texas ranchers began opening other trails, heading west and north to deliver starter herds to new ranchers along the Colorado section of the Union Pacific. The most important of these routes was the Goodnight-Loving Trail, which was established by the tough Texas veteran Charles Goodnight and his partner Oliver Loving. In 1866 Goodnight and Loving gathered about 2,000 steers at the Brazos River and started southwest. At Fort Sumner, New Mexico, they sold some 1,200 head to the Army. While Goodnight, vastly encouraged, went back to Texas to get more cattle, Loving turned north from the fort and sold the rest of the herd near Denver to an ambitious stockman named John Wesley Iliff, who had a contract to supply beef to the Union Pacific's tracklaying crews.

By 1867 Iliff was doing a land-office business in Texas steers. To supply beef efficiently to the Union Pacific, he followed the advancing rail crews into Wyoming, setting up a string of small ranches. For a number of years he annually bought 10,000 to 15,000 longhorns from Goodnight and other Texas drovers. So did many new ranchers along the railroad. Soon cattle from the new ranches were being shipped north and east to stock still newer enterprises in Montana and the Dakotas.

Besides moving cattle to new ranges, more and more Texans found a reason to move themselves. To meet the Easterners' demands for better-quality beef, they began resting and fattening up their trail-worn herds on rented prairies near the railheads before offering them to buyers. The leasing of grasslands was so successful that various Texans bought acreage, set up "feeder" ranches and even grew corn to "finish" their steers. Gradually, the convenient feeder ranches in Kansas, Colorado and Wyoming became home base for a sizable number of Texas cattlemen.

Some ranchers left Texas in disgust with postwar conditions there. During the Reconstruction period, the Lone-Star State was run haphazardly by a Republican carpetbagger government that Texas Democrats—Richard King among them—hated passionately. With courts and law enforcement languishing, organized rustlers ran rampant, and bloody frontier feuds raged unchecked for months and even years.

In spite of the ranchers who moved away, the ranks of Texas stock raisers swelled rapidly, and so did their holdings. New ranchers flocked in, setting up spreads in eastern Texas as far as Fort Worth, pushing north in the Panhandle as the last Comanche war bands surrendered and were deported to a reservation in federally administered Indian Territory above the Texas border. The great empty Northern Plains were stocked so fast and so heavily that by the mid-1870s big operators like Charles Goodnight began renting grazing land from the selfsame Comanches and other reservation tribes. All in all, the Texas cattle kingdom was so immense and productive that in 1880, after disseminating five million steers in 15 years, it still had on hand herds totaling another six million.

At Santa Gertrudis, Richard King had both success and trouble in the hectic Reconstruction decade. His ranch had emerged from the war virtually intact and stronger than ever. The Santa Gertrudis started 1866 with some 84,000 cattle on 146,000 acres. He started making annual cattle drives to Kansas railheads after the war; they grew steadily in size until they totaled 60,000 head in 1875. At last the ranch was paying for itself—and then some.

King capped his personal saga in 1870 by becoming the sole owner of the Santa Gertrudis. This proud event was the result of an amicable agreement with Mifflin Kenedy to dissolve their partnership in the ranch in order to simplify the problems their lawyers eventually would face in settling their estates. Kenedy began ranching on his own as King's neighbor with a starter herd that included some 25,000 cattle from the Santa Gertrudis.

Perhaps the best index to King's success was his ability to overcome livestock losses without breaking stride—indeed, even while expanding. In the first three postwar years King lost more than 15,000 cattle to rustlers; in the next three-year period he lost 34,000 more. By 1876, when the rustlers were finally squelched, King figured that they had stolen well over a million dollars worth of his stock.

For the most part, the rustlers were Mexican outlaws who operated in small bands from hideouts south of the Rio Grande. Their postwar resurgence was triggered by the Big Drift, which brought tens of thousands of untended cattle within easy striking range. The outlaws got rich, and after the jumbled herds were sorted out, they got even richer raiding the ranches between the Rio Grande and the Nueces, driving the stolen cattle back into Mexico to sell for two to four dollars a head. Juan Cortina, organizer of the largest robber bands, preached to the outlaws that their thievery was a kind of national revenge against the hated Texans, and some of their raids turned into orgies of bloodletting. Federal commissioners from Washington reported that "Old and young were subjected to every form of outrage and torture, dragged at the hooves of horses, burned and flayed alive, shot to death or cut to pieces with knives."

King's well-manned, heavily fortified ranch compound seemed strong enough to withstand an outlaw attack. But the captain could not patrol all of the distant boundaries of his huge property. Bandits made off with his cattle practically at will, and they, not lawmen of any sort, policed the roads.

King often had to make business trips between the ranch and Brownsville, and, he said, "I had to travel fast. My life depended on it." But he solved the travel problem in his usual way, by careful planning without regard for expense. At 20-mile intervals along the 125-mile route, King built small relay stations where expert riflemen were posted to guard corrals of fresh horses. For each trip King secreted his funds—sometimes as much as $50,000 for payrolls and purchasing land—in a steel safe built into his stagecoach; he rode inside with a shotgun at the ready and was escorted by half a dozen armed riders. King's bodyguards thwarted several ambush attempts, although one evening a band of Mexicans riddled his stagecoach, killing a traveler to whom he had given a ride.

Many of King's neighbors abandoned their ranches and moved to nearby towns. But King held on grimly, defying Cortina, who had vowed to hang him. In February 1875 the Santa Gertrudis was attacked by a large force of Mexicans who killed several ranch hands and took a large herd of horses. Next month, *Los Kineños* beat off a determined siege. At about the same time, 50 brigands swooped down on a village 12 miles from Corpus Christi, killing one man, hanging another, and stripping and torturing several prisoners. Inflamed by these atrocities, Texas militiamen went on a rampage of their own, murdering innocent Mexicans, and looting and burning at random.

These last atrocities finally prompted the Texas state government to take action. The Texas Rangers, disbanded since 1860 because of certain highhanded activities, were re-established under the command of King's old friend Leander McNelly. Working on tips from cooperative Mexicans, Captain McNelly and a few dozen Rangers launched a series of counterraids. They caught bandits stealing cattle, killed them in running gunfights and dumped their bodies in Brownsville's market square as a warning to their comrades. McNelly even invaded Mexico to get back stolen cattle, and more than once his men had to fight a pitched battle with bandits before they could get away.

The Ranger raids soon had a pacifying effect. The bandits were demoralized, and by the end of 1875 most of them had found safer ways to make a living. With the rustler troubles behind him and with the cattle market booming, King in the next eight or nine years built up his ranch into a 600,000-acre empire worth, in his estimation, about $6.5 million. The growth of the Santa Gertrudis was steady and solid; King, with more than enough capital to indulge in runaway expansion, resisted the temptation to splurge and watched with skeptical interest as other Texans created ranches larger than his.

The captain did stay in the vanguard of ranching innovators. He pursued his systematic program of stock improvement, importing large numbers of Eastern beef cattle and the best Kentucky horses that money could buy. By 1874, when other Texas stockmen viewed with horror and rage the introduction of barbed-wire fencing, King had long since realized that his herds could not be upgraded unless and until their breeding was strictly controlled in fenced-in pastures. In fact, several years before barbed wire was invented, he had begun building wooden fences around 65,000 acres at an estimated cost of $50,000. And to get his herds to market more effec-

Henrietta King and her son-in-law, Robert Kleberg, inspect the ranch's first artesian wells, which Kleberg located and tapped in 1899.

tively, King worked out a bold variation on the trail-drive methods of the day.

Most stockmen, unwilling to strip their ranches of riders to conduct their own trail drives, hired professional drovers for a flat fee or sold their herds outright at the ranch. King did neither; instead, he selected trusted men of proven ability—many of them his own foremen—and put them into business as limited partners. King devised a profit-sharing contract that gave each drover plenty of incentive to do his best work, and yet guaranteed the ranch a tidy profit even if a whole herd was lost en route to market.

For a typical trail drive in 1875, King called in one of his veteran foremen, John Fitch, and sold him a market-ready herd of some 4,700 steers. The contract they signed obligated Fitch to pay King $12 a head and guaranteed Fitch 50 per cent of the difference between the ranch price and the eventual sale price in Kansas. Fitch got the herd to Kansas with very light losses and sold it piecemeal for the current market price of $18 a head. For a few months' work Fitch netted $5,366—more than an experienced foreman normally earned in four years. The herd's sale brought King exactly $61,886.40, all profit except for the modest cost—approximately two dollars a head—of raising the cattle for about four years.

Under this profit-sharing arrangement, King sent as many as 60,000 cattle a year to market. By 1884 King's ranch income was simply too huge to plow back entirely into more cattle and prairie land. The captain diversified, acquiring important interests in the Corpus Christi *Free Press*, a stagecoach line, an ice-making plant and the Corpus Christi, San Diego & Rio Grande Narrow Gauge Railroad Company.

Now the Santa Gertrudis was not just an enormous ranch, it was an institution, known as King's Kingdom. A King herd was instantly identifiable for its superior steers and its proud cowboys on vigorous mounts. Richard King in his mid-fifties was no mere stock raiser, he was the "King of Texas" and the "prince of ranchmen." The Captain enjoyed his wealth and power and used them freely with delight and arrogance. In visits to his banks and agents in New York and St. Louis, he demanded—and got—royal treatment. He threw his weight around in stockmen's associations and in Democratic political circles.

He was, said a veteran cowhand with nice Texan understatement, "a very noticeable looking man."

Despite his advancing age, King was still physically strong and ready to fight at the drop of a ten-gallon hat. One day at the Santa Gertrudis, a big ranch hand named Kelley objected to an angry reprimand from King. "If you were not such a rich man and a captain," he declared, "you wouldn't cuss me as you do." King's retort: "Damn you, forget the riches and the captain title and let's fight!" They did so. For half an hour, the story goes, they wrestled on the bloody floor in a ranch slaughterhouse. Then, exhausted, they shook hands in mutual admiration and walked away.

For all of his flamboyance, fame and powerful friends, King knew himself for what he was, a working man born and bred, and he liked nothing better than associating with others of his kind. While doing his rounds on the Santa Gertrudis, he would stop his buckboard and climb down to talk with his foremen and ranch hands—often about business, of course, but just as often for rough jokes and sporting conversation. When he had an evening to spare in Brownsville, King liked to spend it in Celestin Jagou's inelegant saloon. There he would talk with animation and listen with interest to dock hands and cowboys, and if a drinking companion told him a hard-luck story, King would offer him a personal "loan." King himself favored a brand of whiskey named Rose Bud, and he contrived to keep a jug of it close at hand.

Sometime in the autumn of 1882, King began suffering from a grabbing pain in his gut. The Rose Bud eased it temporarily and he silently bore the pain for more than two years. Then a doctor in San Antonio told him that he was dying of stomach cancer.

King began putting his affairs in order. His main problem was selecting a successor. His younger son, Robert E. Lee King, had died of pneumonia while attending college in St. Louis. The captain looked beyond his surviving son, Richard, whom he set up with his own ranch. He wanted a man who knew the methods, financing, laws and infighting involved in big business. King's attention focused on Robert J. Kleberg, a brilliant young Corpus Christi attorney whom he had recently hired. It happened that Kleberg and King's daughter Alice liked each other, and in October 1884 Kleberg asked for permission to marry

In tribute to her late husband, Mrs. King included his portrait on their ranch's business letterhead, together with a drawing of Texas longhorns bearing the well-known Running W brand of the King Ranch.

her. That settled the Santa Gertrudis succession.

In November of 1884 King hauled his pain-wracked body to St. Louis for the first National Convention of Cattlemen. From what he learned there, his best hopes for the industry were not misplaced. Cattlemen from everywhere in the West, along with their Eastern financiers, were riding high, wide and handsome, and stock raisers in Texas reported that their operations were expanding faster than ever.

The small Texas ranchers were merely getting large; Colonel Kit Carter, who usually ran only 8,000 head on his modest ranch in Palo Pinto County, had bought 40,000 acres more and stocked them with 15,000 head. The big Texas ranchers were getting gigantic. Christopher Columbus Slaughter was buying land that would become an empire 50 miles wide and 80 miles long. Charles Goodnight had just added 170,000 acres to his Panhandle domain, and it was still not enough. He and other northern operators were leasing more grazing land in Indian Territory; they were lobbying so hard to buy land there that Oklahoma, as it would come to be called, was eventually opened to white settlers.

But storm signals were flying, and the cattlemen's convention discussed some of them, too. A stock-man's newsletter had just noted weakening cattle prices and warned its subscribers, "If you have any steers to shed, prepare to shed them now." A Fort Worth rancher told of a small disaster that would soon become commonplace throughout the West: he had overstocked his 100,000 acres with 25,000 cattle, and as a result 15,000 of the undernourished animals had died during a cold winter that well-fed cattle might have survived. But the cattlemen had overcome many such setbacks, and they divined no general pattern worthy of alarm. Their mood was a jovial, spendthrift one.

Richard King made one brief speech to the convention, recommending that the stockmen chip in to buy land for a cattle trail from Texas to the Dakotas, cutting through the growing maze of barbed-wire fences. The cattlemen listened respectfully but tabled King's proposal until the U.S. government paid for the land. King left St. Louis and went home to die.

Early in 1885 King's wife and daughter Alice persuaded him to put himself under the care of his doctor in San Antonio. When he left the ranch for the last time, the captain gave instructions for one of his managers in a matter involving some land near-by. "Tell him," King said, "to keep on buying."

The social register of proud ranchers

The common image of a pioneer rancher's life on the 19th Century frontier as one of unrelieved toil and deprivation was often more fancy than fact. While the life was by no means easy, most ranching families regarded the hard work required to make their spreads grow and prosper as a test of their mettle. Those who managed to exact a good living from the raw country were justifiably proud and grew deeply attached to the land that sustained them.

A fine outlet for the ranchers' pride were the state and county atlases that began to appear about the middle of the century. These illustrated publications showcased the holdings of successful pioneers in lithographs with a sweeping aerial perspective that echoed a 17th and 18th Century European painting technique.

In keeping with the ranchers' romantic view of their land, the results were a charming alliance of fact and fiction. The atlases showed in detail how a ranch functioned; they noted which buildings were used for what purposes, where cattle grazed and where crops were grown. In these pictures each ranch was a small world of almost pristine purity.

Although inclusion in an atlas brought a family prestige, the requirements for entry were far from stringent. The ranch owner paid what amounted to a space fee of up to $60 to give subscribers to the atlas—usually well-to-do ranchers like himself—an armchair view of his home and grounds.

Two horsemen pause to survey the flourishing ranch of J. P. Wiser and Son in Wabaunsee County, Kansas. The Wiser family had come from Canada and listed themselves in an 1887 atlas as "breeders of fine cattle, horses and mules."

SCOTLAND'S GLORY

Ribboned with waterways and stretching almost to the horizon, the entry of John Bostwick of Edwards County in the *1887 Kansas*

GLADIS

State Atlas included two favorite horses. The small house at left is the Bostwick home. Other buildings housed horses, hands and feed.

SOPHIA T. FITZPATRICK

POND

The Fitzpatrick homestead north of Fort Scott, Kansas, was a paean to successful ranching. The artist portrayed a normal workday,

A. FITZPATRICK

with hands training horses, supervising livestock, plowing fields and tending the vegetables and the neat rows of fruit trees near the house.

JOSIAH JORDAN CUSHMAN

The goings on at the Cushman ranch in Churchill County, Nevada, in 1881 fascinate two boys in the road at lower left. An imposing

MARY E. CUSHMAN

residence, the Cushman house had a veranda that wrapped around three sides and had a backyard view of the Dead Camel Mountains.

DAVID M. WIGHTMAN

The Wightmans' 1881 lithograph of their Churchill County, Nevada, ranch shows every hand hard at work. A 12-horse team pulls a

wagon toward the front gate, while a carpenter *(right foreground)* lays planks on a worktable and children cavort near the schoolhouse.

2 | Battling the odds and the elements

"There seems no end to the cold and snow," wrote a Montana rancher in 1887. Cattlemen huddled in their snowbound homes, while the worst winter in memory ravaged their stock.

Though the climate on the Plains was harsher than in the Southwest, Northern beef growers provided no feed or shelter for their animals. Mild winters had lulled them into relying year round on range grass. But a drought in the summer of 1886 left the cattle weak and vulnerable. Blizzards from November until February buried the remaining forage under huge drifts of snow. Hundreds of thousands of animals starved or froze to death. A rancher expressed the common futility: "What can poor cattle do when it is 15 degrees below zero and wind blow-ing at the rate of 60 miles per hour?"

When the weather broke, ranch hands fanned out through gullies piled high with carcasses to measure the di-saster: 60 to 90 per cent of some herds had perished. Cattlemen now realized that the range system was a gamble, as one put it, "with the trump cards in the hands of the elements." But for many of them the lesson had come too late.

In Olaf Seltzer's painting of the devastating winter of 1886-1887, an emaciated Montana herd falls prey to equally desperate wolves.

Small-timers struggling to make the big time

"Why these buildings are called ranches is more than I can say," complained a traveler through the Platte River Valley in 1860. "The proprietors do not cultivate the soil, nor do they raise stock, they have merely squatted along this line of travel for purposes best known to themselves."

The visitor was describing the series of primitive way stations he came upon at irregular intervals in the wilderness west of the Missouri River. They were called road ranches, and though they barely deserved the name, they were the hardscrabble beginnings of what would become in a remarkably few years the booming cattle industry of the Northern Plains.

Well before the great longhorn drives of Richard King and others would come bellowing north from Texas, small road ranchers had started to flourish—or at least survive—in the empty heart of the continent along the migratory trails. Travelers saw them as "generally rude specimens of humanity" who dressed in garments made from elk and deer skins and whose "hair has been suffered to grow, giving them a ferocious look." They were, in fact, brothers in spirit and in blood to the mountain men who had pioneered the paths to the West. Many had themselves been trappers and itinerant traders who had recognized new opportunity in serving the rising stream of westward-bound caravans of ox-drawn prairie schooners. By the time these wagon trains reached the North Platte River and the Green River, heading for California or Oregon, the oxen and horses were footsore and trail-weary. The pioneer families were desperately short of food and almost every other necessity, especially

fresh steers and horses to replace their worn-out stock.

It was to fill these needs (and their own pockets) that one-time trailblazers and failed prospectors went into the business of road ranching. Their places often consisted of little more than a tent or sod hut for the rancher, a wagonload of trading goods, a vegetable patch and a small corral for cattle and horses. Many a family cow, unfit for the hardships of the trail, never made it to the lush valleys of the Sacramento or the Willamette but was turned in at a road ranch for a few dollars or a sack of flour. Often the road rancher would trade a healthy steer from his own stock for two exhausted ones from the trail, which he would then fatten up and trade again.

Trading one for two was an effective way to increase a herd, as some of these shoestring ranchers soon found. One of the first, a former fur trader named Richard Grant, acquired a few head of cattle through trade in 1850 and wintered them in Beaverhead basin, in what is now southwestern Montana. In the spring he drove them to the Oregon Trail where he exchanged them for double their number. Other pioneer stockmen soon joined him in Montana.

These seasonal traders were the first cattlemen of the Northern ranges. Their unprepossessing wayside encampments and winter grazing stations were the earliest Northern ranches; their cattle, Shorthorns descended from Durhams and other European breeds raised in the midlands of America, were the first of millions that came to graze on the open lands that before had known only buffalo and nomadic Indians.

Several of the early ranchers who built their herds on emigrant stock were such successful hagglers that within a few years they became substantial cattlemen, running far more animals than could be traded to westbound passersby. Their big opportunity for major profit came in the early 1860s, when a succession of

In his career as a pioneer cattleman in Montana, Granville Stuart fought Indians, hanged rustlers, started a school, collected 3,000 books and wrote some himself.

Old Piper Dan's road ranch at Tongue River, Montana, was a cut above the average. His rambling log cabin was more commodious

gold strikes brought thousands of miners to the Montana hills, providing a hungry and well-heeled local market for meat. Gold also brought the first competition to what had been the closely knit fraternity of road ranchers. Enterprising men of all stripes descended on the mining camps, determined to make their fortunes in beef rather than bullion.

The newcomers, like the men who had introduced cattle to the Montana ranges, discovered that ranching on the Northern Plains was a rough and risky business for both man and beast. Almost as hot as Texas in the summer, the Plains in winter were forbiddingly cold. Life on the range was primitive, and ranch houses were seldom more than one-room cabins. In rainy seasons leaky roofs required the occupants of some shacks to keep their hats and boots on indoors; in winter driving sleet and drifting snow pen-

etrated the chinks in log walls. Until the sustaining hand of woman began to touch them, most ranchers lived on game and canned goods; they slept rolled up in blankets on the floor or in rough bunks lined with coarse bed ticking stuffed with Montana feathers, as the native hay was called.

The cattle endured the frozen winters as best they could, huddled against the elements in what scant shelter they could find. Many perished when vicious storms pounded out of the north, driving them across unprotected range and covering their forage with layers of impacted snow. Their numbers were further reduced by predators of various kinds. Timber wolves tore into isolated groups of cattle and ravaged the calves. Indians augmented their dwindling supply of buffalo meat by plundering the cattlemen's stock. A more serious threat to property were renegade white

than most such way stations, and Dan, who was a Scottish immigrant, sometimes puffed up a bagpipe serenade for trail-weary visitors.

men who built illegitimate herds by rustling cattle and blurring the brands. Formal law enforcement was sparse, and outraged ranchers were forced, for self-preservation, to declare war on the rustlers. Honest men became vengeful vigilantes who shot and hanged scores of outlaws without quarter.

Singular among the men who fought the odds to establish themselves in Northern ranching was Granville Stuart, who came from Iowa in his teens to hunt for gold and, finding little, turned to road ranching in order to survive. Stuart kept a detailed record of the triumphs and hardships of range life as he lived it and through his published works became Montana's first effective spokesman to the outside world.

Stuart epitomized the ranchers of his era and yet, in many ways, was totally unlike them. A restless, complex and contradictory person, he enjoyed the camara-

derie of the hardbitten men of the hills and earned their respect by outshooting them in tests of marksmanship and sometimes outsmarting them at poker. But he never joined them in their favorite pastime—drinking. He was a self-taught scholar who loved books more than anything in life and had so deep a reverence for learning that he eventually helped found a school and collected a personal library of 3,000 volumes. Yet he chose an unlettered Indian woman for his wife and lived for years in isolated valleys where books were rarer than gold. He was a peaceful man of unbending morals with a profound respect for the law, but when rustlers threatened the survival of his ranch, he led a group of merciless vigilantes to hunt the outlaws down and string them up.

Granville Stuart started his career in Montana as a road rancher and went on to tackle almost every role the swiftly changing Western frontier had to offer: prospector, horse trader, blacksmith, boomtown merchant, cattleman, civic leader and legislator. He made no lasting fortune from ranching or any of his other pursuits, and in that sense he was more representative of his pioneer peers than were those storied few who did become frontier millionaires. When he died at 84, well into the 20th Century, a eulogist saluted him, fittingly, as Mister Montana.

In 1852, at the age of 17, Granville Stuart and his brother, James, who was 20, left the farm lands of Iowa for the gold fields of California. After five years of footloose prospecting that brought them more adventure than profit, they decided to go home for a visit. In the summer of 1857 they started east with nine other men for companionship as well as for protection against Indian attacks. It was while they were camped at the head of Malad Creek about 50 miles north of Great Salt Lake that Granville's destiny was sealed: he was stricken with near-fatal fever and for seven weeks lay too ill to move. Slowly, on a diet of sage tea and rabbit broth, Granville was nursed back to health by his brother.

By the time the younger Stuart was well enough to mount a horse, passing travelers brought news that the Mormons had proclaimed an independent state in Utah Territory, that federal troops were on their way to quell the secession and that the trails ahead were blocked by the "Destroying Angels" of Brigham Young, the Mormon leader. Unable to move either forward to the States or back across the already snow-choked Sierras to California, the young men discussed their quandary with Jake Meeks, an experienced mountain man who was camped nearby and had spent the summer trading ponies and buckskin clothing on the migrant trail.

Meeks suggested that as soon as the footsore livestock he had acquired in trade were fit to travel, the Stuart brothers ride north with him some 200 miles to a sheltered valley in the Rockies where they could winter over and wait out the Mormon War.

Late in October the small party arrived in Beaverhead valley east of the Bitterroot Mountains. Granville recalled with fondness his introduction to the life of a small mountain rancher; winter that year was mild, and the men were snug in their elk-skin tents. Deer, mountain steer and elk were everywhere to be brought down by a hungry marksman, and the camp was always well supplied with meat.

The Stuarts soon fell in with other mountain men who were wintering in the valley. Chief among them was that pioneer Montanan Richard Grant, now a ramrod old rancher whom everyone called "Captain." Grant lived with his family, which included two married sons named John and James, in a comparatively luxurious three-room log cabin about 25 miles down the valley from the Meeks-Stuart camp. The high point of the winter was a banquet on Christmas Day to which the Grants invited their scattered neighbors. The long table in the cabin was covered with a white tablecloth and laden with an elaborate, many-course meal—luxuries rarely seen in the remote mountain valleys. Everyone pitched in to a feast of roast elk and buffalo, smoked tongue, baked beans, fresh bread, chokeberry preserves, coffee and the pudding known locally as blackberry duff.

The Stuarts soon learned the ropes of trading with the Indians, and over the course of the winter they kept up a brisk business with friendly bands of Nez Percés, who owned large herds of horses and were skillful breeders. "The price of a common horse," Granville noted in his journal, "was two blankets, one shirt, one pair of cloth leggins, one small mirror, one knife, one paper of vermillion, and usually a few other trifles." By the spring of 1858 the brothers had acquired 20 horses in trade, which they hoped to sell to the Army at Fort Bridger on a fork of the Green River in what was then Utah Territory.

The Stuarts headed south by way of Deer Lodge Valley where, they had heard, a man named Benetsee had found gold a few years earlier. Road ranchers often turned to prospecting to subsidize themselves during the long winter months when their incomes were nonexistent, and to the Stuarts, despite almost five years of near-misses in California, the lure of gold was nearly irresistible.

Traveling to the mouth of the creek where Benetsee had prospected, they worked their way five miles upstream and dug a hole in a likely spot near the bank. Allowing the creek water to burble into the hole, they washed the sand and gravel—using a tin bread pan

they had brought with them from California—and were exhilarated when their work paid off at "ten cents in fine gold to the pan."

There must, they figured, be a bonanza somewhere in the vicinity. Unfortunately, they did not possess either the equipment or the provisions to stay and try to find it. Nor, when they arrived at Fort Bridger and subsequently at Camp Floyd, south of Great Salt Lake, could they locate anyone with mining equipment to sell. But they did learn that the Mormon War was over and that commerce was flourishing along the migrant trail.

The Stuarts set themselves up as road ranchers at one of the crossings on the Green River and were soon acquiring livestock that had become a burden to the wagon trains. For the balance of the summer of 1858, and for the next two trading seasons, the Stuarts road-ranched, driving their small but increasing herds of horses and cattle back into the mountain valleys for winter grazing. In the fall of 1860, still attempting to supplement their meager income with gold, the brothers drove their stock—60 head by now—to Deer Lodge Valley. There they built a cabin and cut poles for a corral. Nearby was the stream out of which they had panned particles of gold two years before. Their plan was to spend the winter

hunting and caring for their stock and to try their hand at prospecting in the spring.

But again they found no quick fortunes; the joint diary that the Stuarts kept faithfully for many years would frequently announce "tolerable good prospects," only to be followed by such disappointing entries as "washed seven pans of dirt and got six cents, not quite a cent per pan." Their only optimistic inventory came from the corral. On June 9, 1861, Granville was able to report a total of "nineteen young calves, four yearlings, thirty-three cows, fifteen oxen, two young steers, and three bulls." Seasonal festivities became increasingly convivial. On Christmas Day of 1861, the bachelor brothers visited the hamlet of Cottonwood. "Had a fine supper," wrote James, taking his turn at the diary, "and then danced all night till sunrise. There were a few students of toxicology occasionally, but they were well behaved and gave the rest of us no trouble." A week later, on New Year's Day, "everybody went to a grand ball given by John Grant at Grantsville and a severe blizzard blew up and raged all night. We danced all night, no outside storm could dampen the festivities."

The music for these marathons, James Stuart recorded, was usually provided by two violins, and the most popular dance was the quadrille. Both men and women paid considerable attention to their appearance; the men trimmed their whiskers and decked themselves out in their best flannel shirts and beaded buckskin suits, and the women, mostly Indian or of mixed parentage, wore their brightest calicoes, scarlet leggings, plaid blankets and ornaments made of feathers, shells or silver coins. The Stuarts' only complaint was that there were never enough women to go around, and a man with an identifying handkerchief tied around his arm would have to fill the place of a woman in some of the sets.

But nothing could take the place of a female helpmeet around the home; before the severe season ended, Granville and James succumbed to the custom of the frontier and took common-law Indian wives.

Life for the Stuart brothers became more comfortable and at the same time more businesslike—for with families on the way, they had to have a steady income. Late in 1862 they drove their small herd to Bannack Creek and opened up a butcher shop and a

This Montana landscape is one of many sketches Granville Stuart made beginning about 1861. He fostered the work of other artists as well and once hired painter Charles M. Russell as a cowpuncher.

A View of the Gold Creek Looking West.

saloon-grocery to serve the prospectors there. Yet they continued to dream of striking it rich on the veins of gold they felt sure were within their grasp—if only they knew where to find them.

As it turned out, there was considerable gold in Montana. By 1863 major strikes were being made in the general area of Deer Lodge Valley—though not by the Stuarts. Boomtowns sprang up at Bannack, Helena and Virginia City while Granville and James sought in vain for their own fortune. They did, however, begin to prosper modestly in a road-ranching venture with a twist: from their Bannack butcher shop they supplied miners with fresh meat, and with various partners they started a blacksmith shop and dry-goods store at Virginia City and later another store at Deer Lodge, formerly known as Cottonwood, to

meet the fast-growing market for supplies of all kinds.

Unfortunately, they had neither sufficient capital to support their ventures nor enough cattle to satisfy the demand for beef. The opportunity to make a killing from the miners rather than from the mines slipped through their fingers. The same opportunity was seized, however, by a remarkable newcomer to the gold camps, a young man named Conrad Kohrs—who would become first a competitor and later a partner of Granville Stuart in a career that would make Kohrs one of Montana's dominant ranchers.

Born in Holstein, then part of Denmark, Con Kohrs had arrived in Deer Lodge Valley in the late spring of 1862 after a wandering youth spent as a cabin boy, apprentice butcher, sausage salesman, grocery clerk, logger, river raftsman and prospector. He settled in at a mining camp and was about to start

Mountains, from Deer Lodge City.
August 22nd, 1865; No 6

G. Stuart

panning for gold when he met one Henry Crawford, who had decided, like the Stuarts, that feeding the hungry miners was a surer, if slower, way to wealth than prospecting.

Crawford was looking for a butcher and Con Kohrs, the one-time apprentice meatcutter, volunteered. They struck a bargain and Kohrs—with only a crude skinning knife, a bowie knife, a carpenter's saw and a borrowed scale for tools—set up shop as a butcher in the mushrooming town of Bannack. Crawford, meanwhile, scoured the countryside for meat on the hoof to keep Kohrs supplied.

It soon developed that Crawford was overly fond of whiskey and gambling, and Kohrs found himself buying cattle as well as running the shop. Before long, Crawford ran afoul of the chief of the local desperadoes, a hard case named Henry Plummer, who believed that Crawford had information that could send him to jail and must therefore be eliminated. Crawford left town and soon fled the Montana region for good. Con Kohrs had become his own boss.

Hardly had Kohrs inherited the shop than his customers began to scatter, heading mostly for the Alder Gulch district around Virginia City where a new gold strike had been reported. Undismayed, Kohrs packed his knives and headed toward Alder Gulch too, taking on a partner named Ben Peel. Soon the firm of Con & Peel was doing a profitable business with the miners. The partners opened more shops in Helena and acted as wholesalers for other butchers. Kohrs had to ride hundreds of miles a month between widely separated ranches looking for cattle to buy.

To pay for the beef Kohrs often carried gold dust worth $5,000 or more in his saddlebags—an exceed-

ingly risky business in a region that, since the discovery of gold, was swarming with road agents. The gang led by Henry Plummer, with whom Crawford had tangled, was estimated to have killed 102 people before Plummer and some of his men were caught and hanged in January 1864. These bandits were well aware that Kohrs carried large sums of money. To evade capture Kohrs gradually built a network of stations with 12 fast horses spotted along his cattle-buying routes so that he would always have a fresh mount available.

Kohrs's closest call came in the fall of 1863 when he was informed by a friend at a road ranch that two frontier thugs named George Ives and "Dutch John" Wagoner were out looking for him. Kohrs jumped atop a rangy gelding named Gray Billie and hurried toward the safety of Johnny Grant's ranch, keeping out of sight as best he could in dry-water courses and other natural depressions. Soon, however, he was forced to move out into a long uphill stretch of open country—and there behind him, two or three miles off, were a pair of horsemen, moving fast and kicking up a trail of dust.

Kohrs urged Gray Billie on over the Continental Divide and, looking back, saw the two horsemen gaining fast. At the first patch of brush he dumped all his gear to lighten Gray Billie's load and hurried the horse, now caked with dust and sweat, over several more rises, down Deer Lodge Valley and across three creeks. Kohrs and Gray Billie reached Grant's ranch just minutes ahead of their pursuers, having covered some 60 miles in six hours over some of the roughest country in the West. The road agents turned away, but the gallant Gray Billie had run his last race.

It did not take Kohrs long to become one of the most prosperous men in the livestock business. In the summer of 1864—the year Montana became a territory—his road-ranching operation brought in some 400 cheaply bought head of cattle. He experimented in upgrading the Con & Peel stock by importing herds of choice beef cattle from Oregon and also brought in 400 sheep, the first flock to reach Montana. In 1866 when his partner Ben Peel decided to return to the more peaceful climes of Missouri to get married, Kohrs bought him out for $17,500, paid in one solid bar of gold. He also purchased the Grant ranch at

Deer Lodge, the amiable Johnny having decided to move north to emptier spaces in Canada.

Two years later Kohrs married an Eastern bride, Augusta Kruse, and installed her in what was regarded locally as a sumptuous establishment. According to a correspondent for *The Montana Post* of Virginia City, "The dwelling house, which is large and two storied, is by long odds the finest in Montana. It appears as if it had been lifted by the chimneys from the bank of the St. Lawrence, and dropped down in Deer Lodge Valley. It has twenty-eight windows, with green-painted shutters, and looks very pretty."

The interior of the house was less elegant, however, and Augusta—just 19 and newly arrived from Cincinnati—could scarcely have been enthralled.

In this 1887 Charles Russell painting, cowboys pitch camp for a horse roundup near Utica, Montana. Each spring ranch hands made a raucous event of rebreaking horses that had wintered on the range.

"There were no carpets," Con himself admitted. "The floors were all pine and were kept spotlessly white by scrubbing. We had an old homemade bed; strings of rawhide stretched across in place of springs, a straw tick for a mattress." Nevertheless, there were ranch hands to feed, bedbugs to banish, soap and candles to be made, coffee to be roasted, cows to be milked and babies to be born, and Augusta rose to the challenge. She transformed the Kohrs home into a frontier outpost of comfort and style.

While Kohrs thrived, the Stuart brothers were making a living, but not very much more. When in 1871 Granville, who longed to travel, heard that Kohrs was going on a long holiday, he wrote an anguished letter to his absent brother, James: "Con Kohrs & wife start to Germany next week to stay all winter. Good God why cant we make enough to enable us to enjoy ourselves a little, or must we always work for grub and clothes?"

The elusiveness of financial success had not kept Granville from trying his hand at a number of intellectual pursuits. Between his chores as a butcher and a blacksmith, he worked on a manuscript that included a history of the region and its gold strikes, travel itineraries and anecdotes, and a guide to local Indian languages and customs. In 1865 this first book about the new territory was published in New York under the title *Montana As It Is.* The same year, Granville helped found the Historical Society of Montana and served as its first secretary.

At about the time that Granville was most deeply immersed in his literary endeavors, another ambitious man, who would earn a place in Stuart's chronicles, was launching an epic trail drive that was to revolutionize ranching on the Northern Plains. Up to 1866 the typical Plains rancher owned a small herd of Shorthorn cattle; even Con Kohrs's operation was small by Texas standards. In that year, however, Nelson Story brought the first large herd of longhorns from the Southwest, blazing a trail for hundreds of huge herds of Texas cattle to follow.

Nelson Story was born in Ohio in 1838 of tough stock that had pioneered westward from New Hampshire. At 18 he was driving freight wagons between Fort Leavenworth, Kansas, and Denver, a 600-mile

course in the techniques of self-preservation. Like so many others, Story soon fell prey to the lure of gold and migrated to Montana. But unlike most prospectors, Story hit a small bonanza, taking $30,000 worth of gold out of Alder Gulch. And while he was ahead, he quit.

With his grubstake in his pocket, Story looked around at such burgeoning mining towns as Bannack and Virginia City—which by 1864 had a population of 10,000—and noted the trouble that Kohrs, the Stuarts and others often had finding enough meat to supply the expanding market. Story realized that if he could somehow get cheap Texas beef to Montana, he would make a financial killing. By the early spring of 1866 he was in Dallas, where he bought a herd of 600 longhorns at $10 apiece. He then began one of the longest and most arduous cattle drives in history.

On the first stretch of the trail north from Texas, Story, his hired cowpunchers and his cattle confronted the usual, if daunting, difficulties—swollen rivers to ford, Indians who demanded payments for allowing the cattle to cross their territory, thieves and rustlers, and stampedes. Then, at the Kansas border, Story found armed white men barring his way. They were militant homesteaders who were afraid that Texas cattle would infect their own livestock with tick fever. So Story pioneered a new trail around the Kansas settlements until he reached Leavenworth, where he was known and more welcome. From there he pushed westward and finally north, driving the cattle through the desolate North Platte Valley toward Fort Laramie in present-day Wyoming.

The Army commander at Fort Laramie was appalled at the idea that anyone would drive a herd from there into Montana. Directly in the path stood the Sioux and several allied tribes, all in a decidedly hostile frame of mind. Ignoring the officer's warnings, Story armed his 27 men with the latest rapid-fire rifles and headed toward Fort Reno, a new stockade about 140 miles away on the Powder River route.

Before his herd and wagons could reach Fort Reno, Story had his first run-in with Indians. A band of Sioux swooped down, wounded two of Story's cowpunchers with arrows, deftly cut three dozen longhorns from the herd and then galloped away. One of Story's cowpokes named John Catlin was asked

later how many cattle had been lost. He replied, "Not a single head. We just followed those Indians into the Bad Lands and got the cattle back." It was not quite as simple as that. In fact, Story and his men surprised the Sioux in camp and, with their fast-firing rifles, shot the entire band.

Story reached Fort Reno without further incident and left his two wounded men there. He pressed on through more Indian country, often camping by day and driving his cattle by night, and on December 9, 1866, the herd reached Virginia City. The entire drive had taken more than six months and covered almost 1,500 miles. Story had shown the way, though it was a few years before anyone else had the temerity to drive longhorns along the Indian-infested trails from Texas to Montana Territory.

In Virginia City Story found the miners just as anxious for steaks as he had foreseen. He sold a good many of his $10 longhorns for $100 a head. But he carefully kept the best ones for breeding purposes and added to his stock by purchasing the small Short-horn herds of less-enterprising Montana cattlemen.

By the early 1870s Story had joined Conrad Kohrs as one of the dominant cattlemen of Montana, and he was well on his way to becoming a leading business entrepreneur of the Northwest.

Restless, book-loving Granville Stuart had fared less well. His literary skills were bringing him a measure of fame but little with which to stock the family larder. Nor did his various small business enterprises flourish. Then, in 1873, the bottom dropped out of his life: his beloved brother, James, died at the age of 42 of an illness diagnosed as liver disease. James's death, Granville wrote, "leaves a gap in my life that will never close."

To compound Stuart's woes, the bottom dropped out of the national economy too. Obsessed by a dreadful loneliness, unable to make any money, Granville busied himself with unraveling the Stuarts' tangled business affairs and selling off their properties. At the same time he took on an increasing load of civic duties, serving on the local school board, in the terri-

A powerful new lobby for stock-raisers' rights

By 1884 Western cattlemen controlled enough capital to have retired the national debt. To give this concentration of power a unified voice, Colonel Robert D. Hunter, a transplanted Scot, organized and promoted the National Convention of Cattlemen in St. Louis.

It was an impressive affair, attracting more than 1,300 delegates from 34 states and territories. According to a contemporary account, "the ladies, the talent, the wit and the beauty of St. Louis decked their halls and parlors to greet and make welcome the bronzed ranchmen of the plains."

But to the cattlemen, convention business was at least as compelling as drawing-room socializing. In six days of debate the delegates created a permanent organization, the National Cattle and Horse Growers Association of the United States. They also fired off to Washington the first of many resolutions, urging the government to prevent Indians from stealing their stock, finance a National Cattle Trail for cattle drives out of Texas and offer long-term grazing leases on lands owned by the government.

"FIRST NATIONAL CONVENTION OF CATTLEMEN" IN SESSION.

In the flag-draped Exposition Hall in St. Louis, standards identify delegations of attentive cattlemen and the Dodge City Cowboy Band

FIRST NATIONAL

Convention of Cattlemen

—— OF THE ——

UNITED STATES,

AT ST. LOUIS,

TO BE HELD NOVEMBER 17, 1884.

FOR ANY PARTICULARS

Address

A. T. ATWATER,

Secretary Executive Committee,

Room 20 Singer Building,

ST. LOUIS, MO.

in the center of the far gallery.

snow and ice, it uncovered the carcasses of thousands of dead animals. Stuart's cowhand Teddy Blue Abbott recalled counting the losses: "The weather was hot, and the dead cattle stunk in the coulees. Pfew! I can smell them yet. There was an old fellow working with us who had some cattle on the range; I don't remember his name. But I'll never forget the way he stopped, with the sweat pouring off his face, looked up at the sun, sober as a judge, and said: 'Where the hell was you last January?' "

The winter of 1886-1887 came to be called the Great Die-Up, and nowhere was its impact more catastrophic than in Montana. Even the well-run Stuart-Kohrs operation lost two thirds of its stock. Granville Stuart was badly hurt financially and was so appalled by the massive mortality on the range that he resolved to abandon ranching altogether: "A business that had been fascinating to me before suddenly became distasteful," he wrote. "I never wanted to own again an animal that I could not feed and shelter." Nor did he; he left the management of the ravaged DHS herd to Conrad Kohrs and gradually withdrew from the cattle business.

Many of Montana's other major stockmen, Kohrs among them, set about overcoming their losses. Some plowed their remaining capital into sheep, which could graze on closely cropped land. A few drove their diminished cattle herds to newer grazing areas in northern Montana that had not suffered the effects of overstocking. But the more farsighted cattlemen held on by changing their stock-raising methods. They forsook the open range and bought or leased most of their land, which they fenced. They kept their herds small and concentrated on upgrading them, and they grew summer hay for winter feed.

The determined Conrad Kohrs, whose mining interests and other ventures had kept him solvent in rough times, rebuilt his herds at a measured pace and brought phenomenal prosperity to the DHS ranch. But Granville Stuart did not share the wealth. He spent the rest of his life as he had spent his middle years—dabbling in unprofitable pursuits. When death came to him he was in the midst of writing and rewriting his recollections of a Montana long past and of the men who had made good where he—to the extent that success is measured in dollars—had failed.

Last fling for the West's first hunters

Forced onto reservations and deprived of their natural food source, buffalo meat, Northern Plains Indians would have starved or gone on the warpath if the U.S. had not supplied them with beef beginning in the 1870s. Govern- ment agents bought the necessary cattle from local ranchers, who thus had a handy market for their stock.

The Indians claimed the right to kill and butcher the cattle themselves. Ration days were festive occasions, as the Indians, sometimes in war paint, pursued "the white man's buffalo" with whoops and hollers. The result was more slaughter than hunt, but it gave the Indians a last chance to play out a ritual—and ensured them fresh meat.

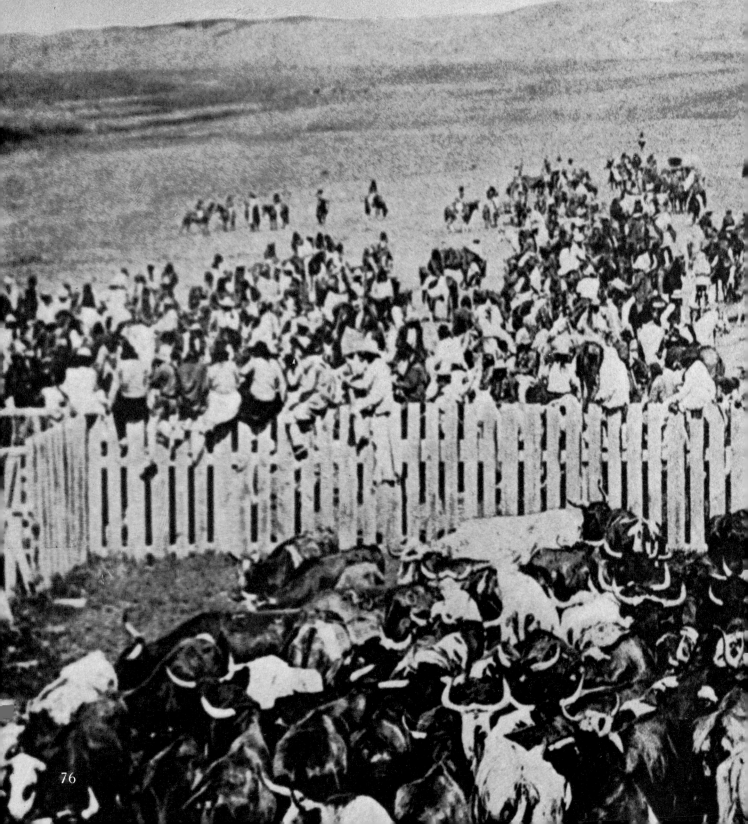

On a beef issue day in the late 1870s, Sioux Indians gather at a cattle pen on the Rosebud Reservation in Dakota Territory, eager to "hunt" their quarry. The Indians made a holiday of this weekly event and government agents complained that while it lasted they neglected their farm work.

Cattle whirl in helpless panic as Indians from the Standing Rock Reservation in Dakota Territory take turns picking them off with Winchesters (one rifleman can be seen in the right foreground). Sometimes the steers were set loose on the range to be pursued by Indians mounted on ponies.

With all the cattle felled, the marksmen enter the corral to claim their kill. By an act of Congress, reservation Indians were each allotted 730 pounds of beef a year—a bonanza for white ranchers who fulfilled government beef contracts.

Under the eye of a government agent *(far right)*, an Indian bends to skin a steer that has received a symbolic *coup de grâce* from the bowman at right. In 1890 the Indian Bureau prohibited the hunt, insisting that beef be issued over the butcher's block—clean, lean and shorn of tradition.

3 | A wave of woollybacks

"One heard of cattle barons and cattle kings, but the underestimated sheepman rarely got within the aristocratic fold," wrote Texan Robert Maudslay, recalling his own experiences as a sheep rancher. As a matter of fact, a sheepman had troubles much more pressing than being slighted by history. His herd was in constant danger of being stampeded by irate cowboys or slaughtered by wolves and coyotes. The life of a sheepman on the wind-swept plains was a far cry from the idyllic image of the Old World shepherd peacefully tending his flock.

For many years sheep raising in the West was left to the Mexicans; American ranchers felt there was something ignoble about the musky odor and incessant bleating of the "woollybacks." But when it became apparent that sheep were more profitable than cattle, the sweet smell of money often overcame the strong smell of sheep. By the 1880s southern Montana had one ranch in five running sheep. When jobs were scarce even diehard cowboys, who scorned all things sheeplike, were not above taking a turn at sheep "rustling"—as the legitimate driving of sheep was called.

In addition to the scorn of fellow ranchers, a sheepman had to put up with the vagaries of the sheep themselves, which included ruining the herder's sleep by wandering off to feed at odd hours of the night. "It is one of their little ways of getting even," explained a South Dakota sheep rancher. But through all hardships the sheepman was comforted by the knowledge that, as one expert observer succinctly put it in 1864, "sheep will pay."

A band of 3,000 sheep—the maximum one man could handle—crosses the Platte River in Wyoming at the turn of the century. Wyoming herds grew from 6,000 head in 1870 to five million in 1900.

The indomitable pedestrians of the hills and Plains

"Wherever the foot of sheep touches," promised an ancient adage, "the land turns to gold." For generations the Spanish in America had demonstrated that the saying was true—at least for those who owned the sheep. From the earliest days of the conquistadors, sheep had been the chief agricultural product of the Spanish West, and the rich men of the region reckoned their wealth by the size of their herds. Eventually Americans, too, learned the truth of the proverb. As pioneers spread westward in the 19th Century, sheep in increasing numbers went with them, supplying their need for food, clothing and cash. Then, at midcentury, the discovery of gold in California set off a historic and unexpected surge of westward migration. Prospectors swarming over the mining camps wiped out local food supplies and still had pockets full of dust and nuggets to pay for more. One practical answer to the demand was sheep—durable, pliant, prolific and mobile. In the wake of the forty-niners, the skies were tinted with the dust of millions of sheep on westward trails.

The men who owned the sheep—established ranchers, speculators and rank amateurs—all hoped to grow rich from the fleece and mutton of their "woolly-monsters," and an impressive number did just that. Before the end of the century, sheep ranching rivaled cattle and mining as the West's leading industry.

Despite its economic importance, the growth of sheep ranching was largely ignored by the chroniclers of the era, who preferred to idealize the hard-riding, gun-toting cowboy and the half-wild steers he tended. Compared with such romantic figures the ragged and lonely sheepherder seemed hardly worthy of notice.

Certainly sheepherding was the least glamorous job in the Old West. The animals were stupid and unpredictable; the most defenseless of all domesticated beasts, they needed tending day and night. And the herder, whether he was on the trail or camped on the outer reaches of the owner's vast spread, had to contend with long periods of solitude. A man learned to handle loneliness or he eventually went mad.

Yet the solitude and responsibility produced a resolute and thoughtful breed of men; many more sheepherders than cowboys rose to become citizens of substance and wealth. And though little praised and often scorned, they were proud of the hard life that had fashioned them. "For God's sake," one of them admonished a writer of a later era, "don't picture a sheepherder with a longhandled crook and a face like Jesus Christ. And don't give him so few as a dozen sheep crowding close to him and licking his hand. Give him a sizable flock of at least two thousand and let them keep at a respectful distance. He was a sheepherder, not a shepherd."

Columbus brought the first sheep to the New World on his second voyage, landing with them on the island now called Hispaniola in 1493. Cortés carried sheep to the mainland as food for his legion during his conquest of Mexico. Coronado and other Spanish explorers and gold-seekers trailed them north to what would become Texas, New Mexico, Arizona and southern California. The explorers left the remnants of their flocks with the priests who had accompanied them north to establish missions.

These first flocks were vastly increased over the years by large bands trailed north by the Spanish dons who settled permanently on huge tracts granted by the king of Spain. Their half-wild little *churro* sheep,

A lone herder and his dogs guard the sheep. Good dogs were so valuable that it was said one herder in the 1880s shot a Montana cowboy dead for killing his dog.

developed in the dry climate of Spain, fattened nicely on the short, curly grama grass that covered large stretches of the semiarid land-grant ranches. Since the region produced little else, sheep grazing soon dominated the economy. Wool and textiles were carried from New Mexico to markets as far south as Guadalajara, Mexico City and Veracruz.

The Spanish sheep spreads of New Mexico were staggeringly large, sometimes covering more than a million acres. Ranching families with names such as Otero, Lucero, Luna and Mirabal tallied their sheep in the scores of thousands; herds of half a million were not uncommon. Don Bartolomé Baca, governor of Spanish New Mexico early in the 19th Century, could boast nearly two million sheep on his 1,282,000-acre grant east of Albuquerque, tended by 2,700 herders who lived on the range all year.

The great Spanish ranches were organized in an army-like pyramid. Almost all the authority rested at the top and most of the work at the bottom, done by large numbers of serflike *pastores,* who tended the flocks for five dollars a month and were in perpetual debt to their masters. A U.S. Army officer traveling through New Mexico during the Mexican War described the condition of the *pastores* he saw on the sheep ranches: "They were miserably clad in tattered blankets, armed with bows and arrows; these and their big shepherd dogs constitute their sole defense, although they are subject to be attacked by Indians, and their flocks and herds by Indians and wolves."

As Americans moved into the Southwest before and after the Mexican War, they started their flocks by purchasing the hardy little *churros,* which they called "Mexican bare-bellies" for their scruffy, top-sided coats. As a rule, the American ranchers also hired Mexican-Indian herders and initially adopted the classic Spanish ranching structure. But most of the big owners quickly found it advantageous to streamline the system. Flocks of 1,000 to 3,000 sheep became the responsibility of an individual herder who, though held strictly accountable for the welfare of his animals, was left pretty much to his own unsupervised devices. For most of the year his only human contact was with the camp tender, who made the rounds of the herders' camps every few weeks, bringing fresh supplies of beans, salt pork, flour, coffee and other staples, along

with books, magazines, old newspapers, mail and messages from the owner-manager of the spread.

After 1800 the sheep-grazing industry also flourished along the East Coast of the United States, strengthened by the introduction of the Merino breed imported from Europe. The improved strains expanded rapidly to the burgeoning agricultural Midwest states, and a few small bands accompanied the early wagon trains over the Oregon Trail in the 1840s. They were crossbred with strong European strains brought to Oregon in ships around Cape Horn.

The census of 1850 recorded 15,382 sheep in the Oregon Territory, a nucleus of fine-looking animals that offered a higher-quality wool than did the *churro*-based flocks to the south. In California, despite a Spanish heritage of mission-based herds, sheep raising had been a diminishing industry since the turn of the century. By conservative count there were fewer than 18,000 sheep in the state in 1850, just as the exploding gold-rush demand created desperate shortages of meat and wool. The few sheep that were available were soon devoured, and even an infusion of quality animals driven down from Oregon could in no way satisfy the demand.

Into this situation moved the shrewd New Mexico sheepmen. For them the gold rush had come just in time. The enormous herds in the Southwest had outgrown the available market and sheep were selling for less than a dollar a head. Some ranchers, like Miguel Otero and Antonio José Luna, gambled early on leaving their home spreads and trailing large herds of their own animals to California. Otero and Luna turned a quick fortune in 1849 by driving 25,000 sheep in 10 closely spaced bands from Santa Fe to southern California, thence north up the central valleys to Sacramento where ore hunters hungrily purchased the animals at prices ranging from $10 to $25 a head.

Other New Mexico ranchers chose to profit more modestly by selling *churros* to speculators and adventurers who were willing to undertake the risks and terrors of the trail. Among those to accept the challenge was a tough and imaginative mountain man named Richens Wootton, who at age 36 had spent half his life roaming the deep West as a hunter, fur trapper, scout and Indian fighter. Now, in the late

"Uncle Dick" Wootton's grim gaze reflects the determination he needed to make a 1,600-mile sheep drive through Indian Territory in 1852. Wootton had no previous experience in herding sheep.

spring of 1852, he saw a chance to earn a substantial fortune in one bold undertaking.

"Uncle Dick," as Wootton was called, proposed to buy a herd of sheep from the overstocked New Mexico ranchers and walk them 1,600 miles to the gold-fevered Sacramento Valley. The miners there, he knew, would have preferred beef, but sheep were cheaper and more amenable to the rigors of a trail drive. They could adapt to rough terrain, could subsist on foliage too sparse for cows and could get along on a fraction of the water needed by cattle. They also required fewer handlers. It took seven mounted cowboys to move 1,000 head of cattle any distance; the same number of sheep could be tended easily by a single herder, on foot, with the help of a good dog.

Wootton had never handled sheep before but he was no stranger to the territory he had to drive them through to reach the gold camps—an uncharted obstacle course of swift rivers, raw mountains and scorching desert populated by hostile Indians. "I knew that there was scarcely a mile of the road," he said, "which was not beset by savages who were making it

their principal business to rob and murder a white man whenever opportunity offered."

For some $5,000 Wootton purchased a band of 9,000 bleating sheep. He invested another $1,000 in provisions, a string of pack mules, eight goats to serve as "bell leaders" for the sheep and, indispensably, a trained sheep dog. He prudently supplied each of the men he had hired to accompany him—14 Mexican herders and eight American guards—with "a first class rifle, a pistol and a knife." But Uncle Dick had little trust in his own men. He worried about "the chances of their failing me at a critical moment, or perhaps planning murder and robbery on their own account."

On the morning of June 24, 1852, Wootton pushed his noisy procession out of the sleepy town of Taos, along the upper Rio Grande and into the mountains north and west. The herders had to coax and bully the skittish sheep across one stream after another swollen by the late spring thaw, but the caravan made steady progress until reaching the San Juan Mountains of Colorado—home of the Ute Indians.

Wootton had dealt with Utes before and was prepared to pay tribute in order to gain passage through their land. But one night a Ute raiding party too impatient for amenities tried to make off with some of the sheep and mules. They were driven off by rifle fire from the guard posted around the herd's perimeter.

Early the next morning the Ute chieftain, named Uncotash, stormed into the camp with a band of warriors and demanded payment for the trespass. Wootton coolly assured him that fair compensation would be arranged at a proper powwow, just as soon as the caravan reached bed-ground along the Uncompahgre River that evening. To demonstrate good faith, Uncle Dick sent a couple of his guards on ahead with the chief and his warriors to pick out a campsite and await the herd's arrival. But the men Wootton selected, unnerved by the company of the most glowering Indians they had ever seen, soon made excuses and fled to the relative safety of the trail group.

Chief Uncotash took the guards' retreat as a personal affront. With 100 men, he galloped back to Wootton and loudly accused him of breaking his agreement, acting, to Wootton's seasoned eye, "in a very warlike manner." The Ute warriors split into

A ram on a Navaho reservation in New Mexico retains a degree of the lean look of its *churro* ancestors. Navahos maintained the *churro* strain long after most sheepmen had bred it out of their flocks.

squads, each squad surrounding and isolating one member of Uncle Dick's frightened crew.

"I had never been so badly scared in my life," Wootton later admitted. "Just at that time I think an old-fashioned Mexican dollar would have bought my entire outfit." The veteran mountain man struggled to maintain his composure. "I tried to pacify and explain to the old heathen, but he kept railing at me," Wootton explained, "until I got mad."

Uncotash should have eased up while he was ahead, for suddenly, to the amazement of both the Indians and sheepmen, the two leaders were rolling on the ground in a desperate struggle. The strongly built Wootton soon got the upper hand; holding his knife at the chief's throat, he demanded instant surrender.

For a taut moment a full-scale massacre seemed to hang in the balance; but Uncotash, the knife point pricking his windpipe, opted for losing face rather than his life. He called off his warriors, and the drive warily resumed to bed-ground at the river. There a peace pipe was passed and Wootton, eager to patch the chief's tattered ego, gave the Indians far more ammunition, flour and other valuables than he had budgeted.

The next morning, having kept one of the Utes in camp overnight as insurance against treachery, Woot-

ton and his band crossed the river and left Ute territory as fast as 9,000 sheep could be made to move.

Wootton managed to get the herd across the trackless barrens of Utah and Nevada. He had a few more brushes with Indians—none as tense as the confrontation with Uncotash—and later averted a mutiny among his own men by ordering six of them out of camp at gunpoint. He moved the sheep over the Sierra Nevada ahead of an early snow and finally down the winding American River Valley to winter pasture at a place called Elk Grove, some 12 miles north of Sacramento. Of his 9,000 head, he had lost only 100—a remarkable survival record for even the most experienced trail herders. In the spring he sold them all for $50,000—10 times what he had paid for them—and returned to New Mexico.

Satisfied to get out with his scalp intact and a fat profit, Dick Wootton made only one drive to California. But his trip told the story of a virtual stampede, mostly by neophytes who had no more experience with sheep than Wootton had and—with a few exceptions—even less knowledge of the cruel country they had to cross. What they shared was a quest for money and a willingness to risk their lives to earn it.

One who followed Wootton's example was the famed scout Kit Carson, who bought 6,500 sheep in New Mexico in 1853 for about $2.50 a head and trailed them from Santa Fe to Sacramento along a route to the north of that taken by Wootton. Carson made $30,000 from his venture, enough money to enable him, for the first time in his life, to build a ranch of his own in New Mexico.

On his way home Carson reported seeing 100,000 sheep on the trail in bands of 10,000 to 25,000, all headed for California. From 1850 to 1860, half a million sheep were trailed to the gold camps from New Mexico alone. Many thousands more survived the even longer drive from the Midwest or the ship voyage from the East Coast around the Horn. By the end of the Civil War more than a million head had reached California and another 100,000 had begun to stock the still largely unpopulated Northern Plains west of the Missouri River.

Early drovers like Carson and Wootton quickly learned that a sheep "trail," particularly on open range,

Prize imports to better the breed

Western sheepmen improved their flocks steadily with experimental breeding. Their original stock—descendants of the *churro* breed brought by the Spanish conquistadors—could withstand the West's severe winters and summertime droughts. But *churros* were small animals—typically, a mature male weighed only 65 pounds—and produced coarse, inferior wool.

In order to develop meatier sheep, the ranchers crossed their animals with various large-frame breeds from the East, most of them of English origin. To improve their wool harvest, they paid up to $1,000 a head for choice Merino rams—another Spanish breed developed especially for thick, silky coats. By the 1870s California crossbreeds, benefiting from the rich grasses and a mild climate, weighed 10 per cent more than Eastern sheep, which lacked the *churro* strain, and produced 20 per cent more wool each year.

A celebrated Spanish breed, the Merino traveled westward with the early ranchers.

91

The Fat-Rumped sheep, imported in limited numbers from the British Isles, was unusually proportioned, with much of its weight in its tail and hindquarters.

New Oxfordshire rams from England cost $250 to $500 and were prized for their silky coats. One phenomenal ram yielded 17 pounds of wool in a single season.

With an undulating set of horns, the Saxon Merino ram was a favorite of breeders for its soft wool. The breed was a German improvement on Spanish Merino stock.

Descended from the Scottish Black-Faced sheep, this shaggy Iceland sheep grew a freakish third horn. The hardy species thrived in rigorous mountain climates.

was little more than a vague generality. A trail herd could usually make 10 to 15 miles a day, grazing on any grass along the way and browsing on available forage at bed-ground. When crossing stretches of desert, some herds bedded by day and advanced in the relative cool of night to minimize dehydration. In a narrow canyon or at a river crossing, the trail might be only a few feet wide; on an open plain with sparse grass, however, a herd of several thousand might spread out and advance on a front five miles wide, gathering together only at the bed-ground site.

As with all attractive gambles, sheep trailing had its quota of losers. An endless array of hazards lay along the way, of which Indians were only the most constant. To miscalculate the location of suitable drinking water was to invite calamity. Frequently the inexperienced drovers projected their trailing schedules on the basis of the sheep's remarkable staying power rather than their own, less formidable, stamina. And the sheep seemed to understand the limits of endurance better than the men who drove them. One speculator who discovered this to his sorrow was Josiah White, who struck out across the scorching desert west of Tucson in the early 1850s with a herd of 4,200 sheep. White had reached southern California when his thirsty animals refused to move any farther in the daytime heat. White and his herders rushed ahead for water to save their own lives and returned to find that Yuma Indians had driven off their entire herd overnight.

Worse fortune befell John Gallantin, a raffish frontier bounty hunter who, until the end of the Mexican War, had made his living by randomly killing Indians—any Indians—and selling the scalps for $30 each to the Mexican government, which had put a price on the scalps of hostile Apaches. Gallantin gambled on slipping 2,500 head of sheep through the very Indian country where he had conducted his bloody craft. He had almost reached California when the Indians evened the score, slaughtering not only Gallantin but also 25 herders whose only offense had been to accompany him. The Indians, needless to say, also appropriated Gallantin's sheep.

Other hazards of the trail could be every bit as deadly as Indians. Stampeding buffalo could scatter a flock almost beyond retrieval, trampling sheep, and sometimes herders, who got in their way. Spring blizzards could wipe out an entire season's crop of newborn lambs. And there was little to compare with the terror of trying to move a frightened herd away from a huge, wind-driven prairie fire.

Similar perils awaited herders moving their flocks across the Plains from Illinois, Missouri and Iowa. Small flocks grazed their way west alongside the lumbering wagon trains of pioneers bound for Oregon and California. In 1858 one such migrant, camped along the Humboldt River in present-day Nevada, was awakened by a horrendous cracking sound from the direction in which his prize ram and 15 ewes had bedded down for the night. The man stumbled out to find his ram dead from a titanic duel with a huge bighorn buck—and his ewes running off into the mountains with the victor. The man jumped on his horse and, after a frenzied pursuit, recaptured the ewes, but only because they were too trail-weary to keep up with the wild buck's swift retreat.

Among the first to attempt the journey from the Midwest with a large number of sheep were a trio of resourceful young greenhorns who came originally from Maine—Llewellyn Bixby and his cousins Benjamin and Thomas Flint. In 1853 the three partners scoured up nearly 2,000 head of sheep from grazers in central and southern Illinois and, with more hope than savvy, prepared to set off for California. Tom Flint, who was also a physician, recorded the drive in a diary that became a catalogue of large and small disasters encountered along the way.

The young drovers started badly: they neglected to obtain a good sheep dog before they began assembling their herd. This meant that an edgy Tom Flint, on horseback, strove to keep both the sheep and himself calm and collected as each newly purchased band was brought out to join the waiting herd on a stretch of prairie near Bloomfield, Illinois.

"Took care of the sheep out on the prairie," Flint wrote. "Something like work, for the sheep were not accustomed to being held in that manner." The partners eventually managed to procure three sheep dogs, along with four hired hands, four horses, two wagons and 11 yoke of oxen.

On May 7, the Flint-Bixby herders ferried their sheep across the Mississippi near Keokuk, Iowa, and

Candlish's movable home on the range

Until the 1880s a sheepherder slept on the ground with snakes and horned toads, or at best on a mattress of brush. Most nights he had to search through the dark for a seemingly flat spot to roll out his blankets. "But where is comfort," wondered a herder, when "a root stump is under the very middle of your bed?"

It was a blacksmith, James Candlish, who first lifted the herder's bed off the rocks and stumps by building it into a wagon. At his smithy in Rawlins, Wyoming, Candlish shod horses and pack animals for local sheepmen. Moved by their complaints of sleepless nights, in 1884 he designed and built the original sheepherder's "home on wheels" from an old wagon behind his shop.

Candlish's prototype was open in front, with an interior canvas flap to block the wind, and was soon seen wherever sheepherders were to be found. Then, in about 1892, the Schulte Hardware Company of Casper, Wyoming, commissioned an improved model that closely resembled the wagons in the accompanying pictures. It had Dutch doors in front, a window above the bed and a cast-iron stove with an oven.

Grateful herders, especially those on the flat Northern Plains, readily adopted the improved sheep wagon. It was warm or cool as necessary, the canvas cover was tall enough so a man could stand, and the door made it possible to keep their dogs either inside or outside.

Some sheepmen, however, had a low opinion of the wagon. Because herders tended to camp in one place for several days, their sheep had to be herded back to the wagon in the afternoon over land they had grazed in the morning. One rancher in Nevada thought this practice was such poor treatment of sheep that, even as late as 1933, he would hire only "tipitent burro herders," who strapped their gear to pack animals, shifted their campsite with the sheep—and continued to sleep on the ground.

A commemorative watch fob that honors James Candlish (center) was issued by the Wyoming Wool Growers' Association in 1909. The top and bottom medals show a sheep and the sheepherder's wagon that Candlish pioneered. A pin on the back adapted the fob for ladies' wear.

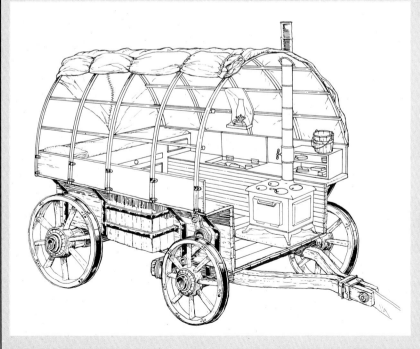

A marvel of compactness, the sheep wagon compressed bunkhouse comforts into a space shorter than a prairie schooner. A bed across the wagon's back bridged a pull-out table, drawers and cupboards; grub boxes, accessible from inside, hung between the wheels. A kerosene lamp and a stove kept the wagon cheery and warm.

Camped alone on winter pasture in Montana, a sheepherder chops firewood for his wagon's stove while his flock grazes nearby.

Grouped sheep wagons signal a rare rendezvous on the range. Herders often met only at lambing, shearing and shipping time.

headed west. Soon they began to attract Indians. A man named James Force was killed as he tried to drive off two Omahas who were stealing a horse. Farther along the trail, as the wagons halted to make camp, "a half dozen Indians bounced out of the brush and commenced to pillage the wagons." The Indians seemed to be succeeding—"the teamsters were scared out of their wits and offered no resistance," Flint wrote scornfully—until they tried to climb into the wagon carrying a formidable woman named Mrs. Johnson, who, with her husband, had joined the party along the route. Furious at the intruders, Mrs. Johnson "went after their hands with a hatchet," noted Flint admiringly, and drove them off howling with pain.

At every turn the march required patience and resourcefulness. When 10 sheep fell sick from browsing on poisonous weeds, Dr. Tom Flint—who had never treated sheep—pulled five of them through by pouring melted lard down their throats. When the tolls charged by ferryboat operators became extortionate—the more so the farther west they pushed—the herders simply found fords shallow enough to swim the sheep across. Trailing down the valley of the Virgin River in Utah Territory, they made a total of 13 crossings without paying a nickel to a ferryman.

Eight months after their departure from Illinois, the Flints and Bixby arrived in southern California, seasoned now in the sheep business and determined to stick with it. They sold their wethers—castrated male sheep—for an average of $16 each, keeping their ewes and purchasing more stock to start their own breeding herd. Their San Justo ranch would become one of the largest and most successful in California. And California itself would in a few years develop a homebred sheep industry sufficient not only to fill its own needs but also to begin a reverse migration of sheep—and sheep ranchers—to the empty grazing lands just east of the Rockies.

While sheep ranching was growing in size and importance throughout the West, the daily life of the sheepherder—like that of the sheep—remained essentially unchanged. Whether moving cross-country or settled on an established range, herding still meant trailing the flock to suitable grass, making camp on appropriate bed-ground, setting the sheep each morning in their

grazing direction and checking for strays, cripples or any abnormalities in behavior. Most important, it meant staying in touch with the indispensable dogs, which not only kept the frisky yearlings from straying but also provided the herder with companionship.

Some of the herder's most exasperating—and often costly—problems involved simply protecting the sheep from their own defenselessness and basic stupidity. If sheep were missing when the flock returned to bed-ground in late afternoon, the strays had to be found before nightfall. A missing animal almost always was dead or in dire trouble, and trouble came in many forms. A sheep might wade into a bog, get stuck and just stand there mute, stoically awaiting rescue or death, whichever came first. A young sheep exuberantly rolling on its back in a new spring meadow might find itself unable to get up, its light, spindly legs incapable of generating enough momentum to roll upright. Merely wading in a stream or pond, a heavily fleeced ewe or wether could become too waterlogged to climb out. Bloat, caused by gorging on the first green foliage, could immobilize an animal and make it easy prey for wolves or coyotes. (A seasoned herder knew exactly where to stick the point of his knife to safely deflate the sheep's stomach.)

Sheep themselves gave no reliable danger signals. Bleating usually meant things were normal. A terrified sheep usually made no sound at all. Adult sheep would stand frozen in silence as they watched a wolf seize and carry off a lamb.

While a sheepman gradually learned the limitations of his charges, his dogs apparently knew about them all along. The earliest Mexican sheep dogs were primarily guards rather than herders, large, ferocious creatures of uncertain lineage trained to protect the sheep against all attackers—writhing, winged, two-footed or four-footed. In the American West, however, most sheep dogs were true herding animals, descendants of the collie-sized Australian shepherds or of smaller black-and-white Border collies originally imported from Scotland and Australia. The herding instinct was deeply ingrained in these breeds, and young dogs were sent out at an early age to learn from their elders how to cope with the wayward ways of sheep. Obedience to the herder and loyalty to the flock were absolutes; exuberant diversions, such as

chasing rabbits, were sternly discouraged; barking was permitted only when essential to warn of danger or to turn or discipline recalcitrant members of the flock. Few sheep dogs needed to be punished physically. "The worst thing you could do to them," recalled one Oregon herder, "was to scold. When you scolded, the dog reacted just like it had a whipping. He would never do it again."

A well-trained dog in action was a joy to watch, sensing any restlessness in the flock, anticipating eagerly the herder's spoken, whistled or shouted commands, which frequently were accompanied by hand signals. A smart dog never nagged or "drove" his sheep but simply persuaded them with his self-assured leadership—a quality few sheep possessed.

A good dog was also invaluable in warning of predators, particularly the coyotes that circled in search of lambs and laggards from dusk until dawn. A herder would jerk out of a sound sleep at the dog's whimpering growl, grab his rifle and fire a shot to frighten off the marauders. He might have to repeat

the process several times before morning, but it saved the lambs. Some dogs, particularly the larger shepherd breeds, could overtake and kill coyotes, which were exceedingly fast and wily animals.

Within the closed society of sheepherders, an outstanding dog would become legendary for its intelligence and bravery, and the descendants of such a dog were sought after for generations. A herder and his dog were inseparable. When a herder died on the range, his dog might refuse to leave his body or even to take enough food to sustain its own life. The attachment was reciprocal. In the strange and solitary life of a herder, the ultimate sorrow could be the loss of his dog. As Joseph McCoy, a 19th-Century chronicler, expressed it: "A shepherd will sigh to lose his friend; groan if his wife or child dies; but if his dog is lost by death, his grief is overwhelming and his anguish cannot be assuaged."

The men who could develop such kinship with a dog while accepting a life of minimal human contact were a complicated breed that sprang from many

A herd of full-wooled sheep is driven into corrals in the fall roundup on a ranch near Billings, Montana, at the turn of the century. Sheep ranching around Billings was spurred by the arrival of the Northern Pacific Railroad in 1882. By the 1890s Billings had become a major depot, shipping more than 15 million pounds of wool annually to the East.

sources. The first of them were of Mexican and Indian stock or some combination of the two. As sheeping grew and spread, they were joined and gradually supplanted by emigrants from Europe—from England and Scotland, Germany and Scandinavia, and the mountainous Basque country of France and Spain. A lesser number were American drifters of assorted backgrounds: refugees from crowded cities, unhappy marriages or drinking problems.

For some the anonymity and, in its way, the stability of the herder's life was the attracting force. Others saw it as a way, albeit a hard one, to make their fortune through the *partido* system, a method of profit sharing that had its roots in Mexico. Most of the early Mexican *pastores* were simply hired hands, but on a few ranches where the owners could not afford a string of paid retainers, flocks were tended on shares by herders who received payment in kind. If such a herder was lucky and skillful enough to avoid the kind of disaster that could wipe out his herd, he would each year become the owner of an agreed percentage of the herd's increase—the newborn lambs—and he would gradually build up a flock of his own.

As the sheep industry mushroomed in the cash-poor American West, the *partido* system became widespread. It assured the rancher that the herder had a strong incentive to take good care of his sheep, and it enabled the herder to keep always in his mind's eye the tantalizing vision that he might one day become an independent rancher himself.

The required characteristics of all herders were bravery, self-sufficiency and a dedication to the well-being of the sheep—though not necessarily a fondness for them. Above all, the herder had to be able to accept and adapt to his own company—exclusively—for weeks and months at a time.

Unlike the cowboy, who took an extravagant pride in flaunting the wide-brimmed hat, decorated chaps and tooled-leather saddle that were the badges of his profession, the sheepherder, even one with money in the bank, rarely bothered about his attire. For long periods, after all, he had no one to get dressed up for and no place to go.

Texas sheepman Robert Maudslay said his shoes were "run down so much on one side that the uppers were constantly threatening to become lowers, and the soles seemed always aspiring to become uppers on the opposite side. Sometimes when I was assailed by a fit of economy I would change feet and use the right shoe on the left foot and *vice versa*." His socks, Maudslay noted, "were sometimes socks and sometimes a piece of oat sack wrapped around my feet."

If his trousers lost a button or suffered a rip, Maudslay made repairs with a mesquite thorn. "But there always came a time," he admitted, "when a patch became imperative, and this I would put on with needle and thread and a piece from a discarded pair. If the patch wore out, I would patch the patch, and if that wore out I would even sometimes patch the patched patch. But I never allowed myself to go further than this.

"My underclothes? I hadn't any," Maudslay said. "In the wintertime I used to double up and make my summer top garments become the under garments for winter use. As for my hat, really it was more than a hat; it was two hats in different stages of antiquity. One was minus a brim and the other minus a crown, but the two together formed a fairly complete head covering. If they had been of the same color, it would not have looked unusual in any marked degree; but one was black, and the other had been white.

"Add a canteen slung across my shoulder," Maudslay concluded, "a rifle resting in the hollow of my left arm, a curved stick in my right hand, and you have a pretty accurate picture. I weighed a good, solid one hundred and fifty five pounds, was as sun-tanned and weather-stained as anybody could be. I could lift a sack of salt weighing two hundred pounds and put it into a wagon alone; and once I threw two thousand sheep of all sizes into a dipping vat in five or six hours without aid from anyone."

Wherever the herds trailed or grazed, herders would leave testaments to their solitude: tree trunks in the remotest groves of aspen were etched with initials, dates, obscenities and, occasionally, some truly intricate bas-reliefs of female figures, religious motifs and cryptic abstracts. High piles of stones, some in amazing configurations, loomed over desert knolls and mountain ridges to further attest to the herders' endless battle against boredom.

Many herders read voraciously, almost frantically, everything they could lay hands on: old newspapers,

The Basques: dedicated herders from the Pyrenees

Sheepherders were men from many nations, often new arrivals in the United States. None were more pervasive, and successful, than the Basques, a proud and ancient race from the Pyrenees Mountains between France and Spain.

The Basques spoke Euskera, a language that is unrelated to any other European tongue. Many had been shepherds at home, and the first of them migrated to South America a century or more before the gold rush lured them to California in the 1850s. Once there, the Basques discovered that the experience of generations of their forebears enabled them to make a living by herding sheep, and some were able to send for their brothers and cousins.

Eventually, many became flockowners in their own right. Their method was slow but simple: a herder would take part of his pay each year in ewes, running his sheep with those of his employer. When a diligent herder accumulated a large enough flock he went into business for himself, grazing the sheep wherever he could — often on public land.

By 1900 Basques had spread across the Plains and mountain states, often establishing their own communities. In California, where they had made their start, two thirds of the members of the state woolgrowers' association were Basques.

It was said that "the word of a Basque is as good as a written contract," but with their limited English and clannish ways, they were not universally popular. An Idaho newspaper in 1909 denigrated them as "filthy, treacherous and meddle-some" though it admitted that "they work hard and save their money."

The sheepman's life was always solitary but it was especially lonesome for the immigrant Basque who had no family with him. Stories abounded of Basque herders who, despairing of ever seeing their loved ones again, committed suicide or went insane. But most survived the hardships and solitude.

They left a legacy of independence and dedication to their four-legged charges best dramatized in the story of a lone Basque who discovered that a black bear was in the midst of his sheep. He sent his trusty dog to scare off the bear, but with a swipe of its paw the bear killed the dog. At this the herder abandoned caution, unsheathed his knife, strode in and cut the marauder's throat.

Basque sheepherders and cowboys (wearing neckerchiefs) gather at the Pioneer Saloon in McDermitt, Nevada, around 1900.

103

dog-eared novels, Shakespeare, back issues of the *London Illustrated News*. More than one immigrant herder taught himself to read English with the help of a Sears Roebuck catalogue. For lack of anything better to read, one Texas sheepman took a copy of *Webster's* dictionary to camp with him. He found it so fascinating that he pored over every word from cover to cover, then started again at A.

Strangers were amazed at the learned character of an average herder's conversation, once the barriers of reticence and language were overcome. Reading afforded the herder an escape from loneliness and helped him forget such discomforts as wetness, freezing feet, thirst and the incessant blather of his herd.

Bill Leonard, who spent his youth among the flocks on the plains of eastern Oregon, confessed: "I never did like any part of the sheep business. The baaing and baaing and baaing was just too much." Nor was bleating the only sound: Archer Gilfillan, an

old herder from Dakota, actually catalogued his recollection of herd noises. He said they included coughs, gargles, wheezes and a "noise like a three-weeks-old baby choking to death on spaghetti."

Gilfillan also thought the herder's life was a hard one. "The wonder," he said, "is not that some are supposed to go crazy, but that any of them stay sane."

Yet some sheepmen scoffed at the assumption that solitude automatically induced depression. "There was too much to do, too much to look at, too much to read, too much to think about, for loneliness," argued Robert Maudslay. "I've been lonely in big cities, but never on the range." Another veteran herdsman, Arthur Chapman, agreed: "The herder knows the ways of the wild things of mountains and prairies and his hours of solitude give him a contemplative cast of mind which one finds in few men today."

Nevertheless, the feeling of being alone in an empty, inhospitable world could sorely test a man's

expected to fleece up to 100 sheep per day, which led sheepmen to remark that "A shearer is a herder with his brains knocked out."

senses. "It happened mostly in the deserts," said Dominique Laxalt, a Basque sheepman who arrived in Nevada from the French Pyrenees when he was 16. "If a man was unlucky enough to be sent there when he first came, it was a terrible shock." Laxalt described his own battle with homesickness and depression on his first herding assignment, alone in the desert with a dog and 3,000 sheep: "I can remember waking up in the morning, and as far as I could see in any direction, there were only sagebrush and rocks and runted little junipers. In the first months, how many times I cried in my camp bed at night—remembering the beautiful green Basque country. In the summer, the desert burned your lungs, and every day you had a scare with rattlesnakes and scorpions. In the winter, the blizzards tore at you and soaked you so that you were wet and freezing day and night.

"Those first few months, you thought you would go insane," Laxalt concluded. "Then suddenly, your mind turned the corner and you were used to it, and you didn't care if you ever saw people again." Laxalt survived the lonesomeness of herding sheep until he was nearly 80. One of his sons became governor of Nevada and later a United States Senator.

The few brief weeks of the herder's year when he did have the companionship of other sheepmen were also those in which the work load was the heaviest. These were the seasonal exercises of lambing and shearing. The critical lambing time came first—in late winter or early spring, depending on the latitude and elevation of the range. One participant called it "a month-long hell of worry and toil," for the very future of a sheep ranch depended on the number of ewes that gave birth to live lambs and the number of those lambs that could be brought through their critical first weeks and then successfully weaned. Pregnant ewes had to be segregated into "drop bands," watched day and night

A festive sheep-shearing contest at Beatrice, Nebraska, in 1877 is depicted in this contemporary engraving. The winner of the annual competition was the rancher whose sheep yielded the fullest fleece.

and attended quickly; they were not only more defenseless than usual but also more confused. In the event they had difficulty giving birth, the herder became the midwife.

Young ewes were indifferent mothers. Frequently a ewe would fail to recognize her newborn offspring and would amble blithely off to graze, oblivious of the lamb's tottering efforts to catch up and make contact. In such cases, the herder would grab the delinquent ewe with a long-handled sheep hook and tie her to a sage or piñon bush so her lamb could start nursing. Another method, regarded as surer by some sheepmen, required the herder to hold the ewe between his knees, wrap one of his arms around the sheep's neck and with the other hand guide the lamb to its mother's udder, perhaps squirting a little milk in the lamb's face to give it the idea. On big ranching operations the ewe and her offspring might be confined in a compartmentalized wagon or a tent just big enough to hold them—a method that afforded the lamb warmth and protection and forced the ewe to let the lamb nurse.

When all else failed, a good sheepman functioned as an adoption agency. A lamb born to a "dry" ewe could be saved by introducing it to a foster mother or feeding it formula—milk, water and molasses—from a bottle. The care of such rejected or orphaned lambs, known as bummers, was a major preoccupation of the herder, for every survivor represented a future return in wool and mutton. A brand-new bummer was rubbed briskly with a rag until dry, then wrapped in a blanket or heavy cloth and bedded by the campfire with occasional feedings of warm formula. If a ewe with ample milk gave birth to a still born lamb, the herder's immediate task was to get her to accept a foster offspring, whose real mother might either be dead, dry or overtaxed with twin or triplet births. To accomplish this required a bit of subterfuge called "jacketing." The herder would quickly peel the pelt from the dead lamb, shake it right side out and pull it, sweater fashion, over the bummer's torso. The smell of her own offspring clinging to the jacket made it easier for the ewe to adopt the orphan as her own and allow it to nurse. After a few days the relationship was fixed, and the jacket could be removed.

The true social season of the sheep industry came later in the spring, after lambing, when the shearing gangs moved in to remove the heavy coats the adult sheep had grown over the winter. On any sizable spread, the shearing was done by itinerant crews of specialists who followed the market for their skills northward from Mexico to the Canadian border. The arrival of the crews always signaled a major break in the tedium of sheep-ranch life—an excuse to gather for socializing, feasting, drinking, gaming and usually a few good fights. The shearers were a flamboyant lot, especially in contrast to the introspective herders.

Sarah Bixby Smith described the arrival of the shearers at the California ranch her father had founded, which by the 1870s was sending 200,000 pounds of wool—the fleece of 30,000 sheep—to market each year in San Francisco: "Shearing began on Monday morning, and on Sunday the shearers would come in, a gay band of Mexicans on their prancing horses, decked with wonderful, silver-trimmed bridles made of rawhide or braided horsehair, and saddles with high horns, sweeping stirrups, and wide expanse of beautiful tooled leather. The men themselves were dressed in black broadcloth, ruffled white shirts, high-heeled boots, and high-crowned, wide sombreros which were trimmed with silver-braided bands, and held securely in place by a cord under the nose. They would come in, fifty or sixty strong, stake out their *caballos,* put away their finery, and appear in brown overalls, red bandanas on their heads, and live and work at the ranch for more than a month, so many were the sheep to be sheared."

Shearing, like lambing, was sweaty, cumbersome work; a good shearer could handle 100 sheep a day, an expert perhaps 150. For every fleece he clipped the shearer received a token, usually worth a nickel, which he converted to cash on Saturday night when the games and the drinking began in earnest.

Once the sheep were shorn, they were dipped and branded, usually by the herders and ranch hands. The dipping was just that—immersion of the sheep in a hot brew of sulfur, tobacco, and assorted herbs and medications calculated to kill any lice, ticks or parasites and to clear up any skin ailments with which the sheep might be afflicted. The dipping vat was a long, narrow trough perhaps four feet deep and filled to a level that ensured the sheep could barely touch bottom. The animals were thrown or forced into the dip

After shearing, sheep are dipped in a strong chemical bath to kill ticks, scab mites and other parasites. The 1890s sheepmen above used long-handled hooks to dip the sheep's heads underwater as they struggled down the trough. Along with sulfur the active ingredient in many sheep-dips, such as the commercial preparation advertised at right, was tobacco, whose nicotine content was toxic to bugs.

at one end, swam or scrambled 15 or 20 feet, and climbed up a sloping, cleated ramp at the other.

After they had dried off, they were branded in a way less painful, if less permanent, than the red-hot iron used on cattle. The owner's mark was usually applied with a wooden stamp dipped in a bucket of black, red or green paint and pressed to the sheep's freshly clipped fleece. The brand image would remain on the tips of the fleece fibers as the wool grew. To make doubly sure their ownership was clear, many ranchers also "earmarked" their sheep, using a knife to mark one or both ears with distinctive combinations of cuts and notches. By using a slightly different mark each year, a rancher could also tell the age of his sheep when separating them later for market.

The sheep crews faced two more spring chores before returning to the grazing range. For sanitary and reproductive reasons, lambs were relieved of all but one or two inches of their tails. This operation, called "docking," followed the lambing season by about 10 days. It was accomplished quickly and cleanly, usually with a heavy knife and a chopping board, or with a red-hot docking iron, which had the advantage of cauterizing the wound.

The final operation, also called docking by some herders because it was done at the same time, entailed the conversion of most of the male lambs into wethers by castrating them. This operation had two purposes: to produce better mutton (just as steers made better beef than bulls) and to improve the breed by ensuring that the ewes would be bred only with prize rams. The wethering operation, at least for young herders, was perhaps the ultimate test of a sheepman's devotion to his calling: the most practical method for removing a lamb's testicles called for the herder to extract them with his teeth while the animal was being held by all four legs in a sort of elevated sitting posture. Though seemingly bizarre, the method was more precise than a single swipe with a knife and ensured the withdrawal of connecting cords. An old world practice, the skill was looked upon as a sort of badge of the order, a proof of professionalism.

By the time all of these essentials of sheep husbandry had been completed, with the related roistering, most herders were more than ready to return to the peace and solitude of the range. In Southern climes a second shearing might be necessary in the fall, but otherwise all that remained to interrupt the basic rhythms of grazing was the breeding season, a period of approximately a month in early autumn when a few rams, normally isolated, were brought in to run with the ewes. Once the breeding was over and the rams returned to segregated grandeur, the herder could move the flock to range at lower elevation and button up for the long winter. Until the warming winds of spring once again signaled the trials and exertions of the lambing season, there would be little—other than sudden 40-degree drops in temperature, blizzards, and prowling wolves and mountain lions—to break the lonely regimen.

There existed one other great threat to the peaceful existence of the sheepman and his flock: the cattleman, who looked first with disdain and then with outright malevolence on the rising tide of sheep and those who ran them. And a rising tide it was, from Texas to Canada. In 1870 there were more than three million sheep on the Pacific Coast alone, and 10 years later the total had climbed to 5.5 million.

By that time, sheep were becoming victims of their own success, encouraging the introduction of livestock to marginal land and eventually attracting farmers, who plowed the best grassland under. As the West Coast ranges shrank, new grazing land was sought to the east, where the Indian and the buffalo had been driven off the High Plains. In the last great American sheep migration, ranchers began trailing their bands eastward to the Rockies and beyond. In 1880 alone it was estimated that almost 600,000 sheep crossed the mountains to Montana, Wyoming, Colorado, Utah, Nevada and Idaho.

But as sheepmen reached the end of the eastbound trails they did not always find the empty, unclaimed ranges that an earlier generation of trail drives had passed through. Instead, they found cattle—some already there and millions more moving in. This time as the range filled up there was no place else to go, no more virgin land to trail to. Cattlemen and sheepmen rushed to beat each other to what was left of the grasslands and good water. A collision was inevitable, and the cattleman's angry unwillingness to share what he considered to be his rightful and exclusive domain led to decades of brutality and terror on the range.

Montana sheep rancher and state legislator George W. Burt and two of his children hitch a ride behind their steam-powered tractor shortly after 1900. The tractor is hauling 65 sacks of wool from the Burt ranch at O'Fallon Creek to the Northern Pacific Railroad depot at Terry, Montana.

4 | War over land and water

"Whereas, we the pioneers of this Sun River Valley, having established ourselves here at an early day and prior to all others . . ." Thus began the preamble of an 1879 resolution to preserve the Montana range exclusively for cattlemen. Though no individual rancher signed the inflammatory document, it expressed their deepest conviction: getting there first gave them inalienable rights to the land.

Legally, the argument was claptrap. The range was, for the most part, public property. But the reasoning went unchallenged for decades, as long as ungrazed valleys remained to be claimed. Inevitably, however, choice land became increasingly scarce until, by the 1880s, newcomers to the West had no alternative but to challenge the oldtimers' prerogatives.

Friction over access to the range led to extreme solutions. Cattlemen's associations unilaterally declared sections of land fully stocked with beef and therefore closed. By the early 1880s barbed-wire fences snaked across the range, only to be cut by irate neighbors or removed by a court edict. Fury erupted over "appropriated" water holes, grazing rights and transit across the Plains.

Cattlemen fought among themselves and with farmers, who fenced in the open range and plowed the ground under. But the most protracted violence raged between cattlemen and sheepmen, whose swelling herds of sheep could ruin a crowded range. The result was a generation of conflicts like the brutal incident portrayed at right.

Night-raiding cattlemen hold half-asleep sheepherders at gunpoint as their accomplices destroy the defenseless sheep. In Colorado and Wyoming such slaughter sometimes annihilated entire flocks.

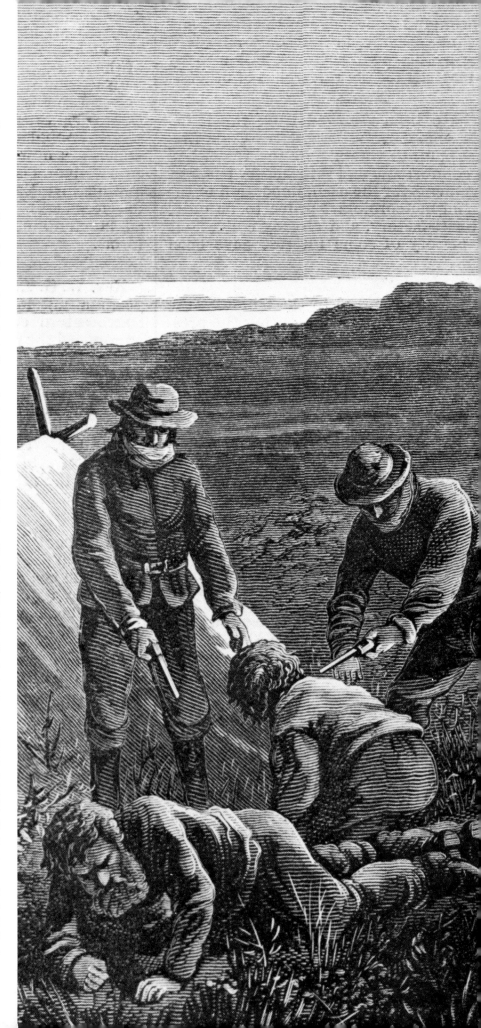

Gunnysackers, rim-rockers and a reign of lynch law

Three hours after sundown one August evening in 1905, ten riders gathered on a rise above a sheep camp on Shell Creek in Wyoming's Bighorn basin. Quietly they covered their faces with bandannas, and at an agreed signal they galloped screaming and shooting into the camp. As the terrified sheepherders tumbled out of their wagons, the masked riders accused them of dawdling on their way to pasturage in the Bighorn forest reserve and told them that their flock of 7,000 had destroyed a range claimed by local cattlemen. Handed a few provisions and ordered to leave the area and not come back, the sheepherders scuttled off, grateful to be alive. Then the riders set about shooting, clubbing and dynamiting to death 4,000 sheep. Lest the sheepmen fail to absorb their lesson, the raiders also shot a team of valuable horses, set fire to the wagons and, as a hideous final touch, tied the herders' sheep dogs to the wagon wheels where they were roasted alive.

The owner of the sheep, Louis Gantz, sought no redress for the savage raid. Like many sheepmen before him, Gantz faced overwhelming opposition in both fire power and public sentiment as long as he grazed his flocks in cattle country like the Bighorn basin. Describing the incident, a local newspaper editor pointed out that "it was well known who perpetrated the heinous deed"—but nothing was ever done to bring the raiders in.

More times than most cattlemen cared to admit, variations on this appalling theme were rung all over the High Plains during the heyday of the open range.

Scattered violence broke out as early as the 1870s as cattlemen contended with one another and with sheepmen, homesteaders and rustlers for control of grass, water and livestock. As more and more men and animals crowded onto government-owned lands, the incidents grew in frequency and ferocity. Eventually, these skirmishes escalated into the range wars that scarred the decades before and after the turn of the century—marking the era as the bloodiest in the settlement of America's public domain.

The bitter conflict over the grazing lands west of the Missouri River was all but invited by the short-sightedness of government land laws. With the Indians and the buffalo contained or driven off in the dozen years following the Civil War, the grass was free for the taking by whoever got his livestock to it first. A pioneer rancher could drive his herd into an empty valley in Wyoming or Montana or Arizona and claim range rights for miles in every direction. But he could not hold legal title to more than a fraction of the land he used.

Under the Homestead Act of 1862, anyone with $10 for the filing fee could enter a claim for a quarter section of the public domain—most of the land from the Missouri River to the Sierra Nevada, with the exception of Texas, which had retained the right to sell off its own acreage when it became part of the Union in 1845. If the homesteader lived on his claim and made a number of improvements, the land became legally his after five years.

For a yeoman farmer in the humid lowlands back East a quarter section—160 acres—was a generous plot, but for a rancher in the high, dry grasslands of the West it was completely inadequate. Cattlemen reckoned that even in good years each steer needed at least 10 acres to graze on. Their view was endorsed in 1879 by a U.S. Geological Survey report that put

Sticks and stones mark the graves of three victims of vigilante justice in an Arizona range feud. Known incongruously as the Pleasant Valley War, the strife claimed at least 25 lives between 1887 and 1892.

115

the minimum practicable holding for a rancher in arid country at 2,560 acres.

Early stockmen simply ignored the land laws. They acknowledged one another's rights to particular stretches of range and water, and newcomers just kept moving until they reached unoccupied space. But eventually the land ran out and ranchers began jostling for grass and water. Canny stockmen filed homestead claims on the banks of streams and paid their ranch hands to file fraudulent claims along the same waterways, for whoever controlled access to a stream controlled the range beyond it, up to the next divide.

Even these measures were no guarantee against the incursions of small-time nesters, whose scattered homesteads broke up the range, or against the predations of rustlers, who found easy pickings among the free-roaming herds. Before long, organized bands of rustlers, attracted by inflated cattle prices, were making big money by driving stray steers into remote valleys, altering their brands and selling them at distant markets. Not infrequently ranchers grew so angry over their losses that they chose not to wait for the ponderous—or nonexistent—machinery of the law to protect them. When one formidable gang of rustlers in Arizona's secluded Pleasant Valley threatened to drive legitimate stockmen off the range, ruthless vigilante reprisals—sparked by a vicious blood feud between two families—all but wiped out the gang, along with a number of innocent wayfarers who happened into the valley at the wrong time.

As much a menace as the rustler, and in the eyes of a cattleman even more contemptible, was the sheepman. A lowly pedestrian among the mounted knights and barons of the Plains, the herder was a peculiar sort who spent months at a time alone with his flock. He generally spoke little English and came from other than Anglo-Saxon stock—perhaps Mexican or Indian or Basque. Or he might be a Mormon, which made him almost as much an alien.

The cattlemen's disdain went double for the sheep themselves, the feeble-minded woollybacks whose habits exasperated even their owners. A Western writer recalled that mutton might occasionally appear on the menu at a cattle-town hotel, but if anyone had the temerity to order it, "the very waiter girls had scorn in their voices when they called to the cook through the kitchen window for a 'plate of sheep!' "

Feelings had not always run so high. In the days when there was plenty of empty range to go around, few ranchers seemed to care what animal a distant neighbor chose to raise. And the vacant grasslands of the High Plains were just as attractive to sheepmen as they were to cattlemen. Sheep from flocks that had been trailed westward out of New Mexico to proliferate in California and Oregon were now trailed back eastward to stock the ranges in the Rockies and beyond. Between 1870 and 1880 the estimated sheep population of Montana soared from just over 4,000 to a quarter of a million, and in all the northern mountain states and territories the figure jumped from less than 200,000 to nearly 1.5 million. By the end of the trail-driving era at the turn of the century, some 15 million sheep had been driven east.

Cattlemen, who in most cases had reached the grasslands first, watched the sheep invasion with growing anger. On the increasingly overstocked range, sheep seemed particularly destructive. It became axiomatic among cowhands that "everything in front of a sheep is eaten, and everything behind is killed." They would surely have agreed with John Muir, the pioneer conservationist, in his characterization of sheep as "hoofed locusts."

It was true that where too many were crowded together or held too long, sheep ate grass down to the roots, and cut and trampled what was left with their sharp, cloven hoofs. In dry areas ground laid bare by sheep would fail to put forth new growth until the next year's rains. Nothing enraged a cattle owner more than a bunch of sheep en route to mountain pasture tarrying on low-lying range, which the cattleman regarded as his own, then moving on to higher ground where cattle could not follow, leaving him "sheeped." To him, a flock peacefully nibbling its way over a rise was no pastoral idyll but a vision of impending disaster. He became convinced that the "woollymonsters" fouled his water holes and tainted the land, leaving behind a smell that made cattle refuse to eat or drink.

It was not long before cattlemen took action to protect their "rights" to the public range. At first they might simply issue a warning to a newly arrived sheepherder to keep on moving. A few cowboys

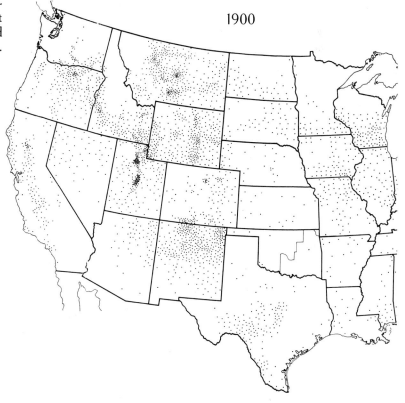

1870

1900

The rapid growth of Western sheep ranching from 1870 to 1900 is demonstrated by the two maps at right, based on U.S. Census Bureau figures. Each dot represents 10,000 sheep. Sheep were already well established in California and New Mexico when the arrival of the railroads in the late 1860s spurred expansion by making it easier to get the sheep to Eastern markets. In Montana, where the 1870 census recorded a grand total of only 4,212 sheep, the 1900 census counted 4.2 million; other sources put the 1900 total at more than six million. This explosive incursion by sheep into land that cattlemen considered their own led to hard feelings and sometimes to open war.

might obligingly direct him around the cattle range, or hustle him through to the other side and bid him a gruff adieu. Soon ranchers and stock associations took to promulgating "deadlines," arbitrary boundaries that sheepmen were ordered not to cross. One of the earliest, and least arbitrary, was established in 1876 by Charles Goodnight, the Texas cattle magnate. After one of his cowhands had wantonly drowned 400 sheep belonging to the governor of New Mexico, Goodnight paid damages and agreed to share the Panhandle with the local sheepmen, leaving them the Canadian River Valley as long as they did not cross the divide into the Palo Duro Canyon. The pact was honored by both sides for many years.

Few such arrangements were so amicable. On most ranges a sheepman crossed a deadline at considerable risk. One Montana sheep owner, edging his band toward what was predominantly cattle country, received a pointed message from local cattlemen: "If you take sheep to Powder River bring your coffin along. You will need it." If a sheepherder chose to ignore such a threat, he could expect even less subtle countermeasures from the cattlemen. Poisons, such as blue vitriol or saltpeter—the latter toxic to sheep but not to cattle—might be spread in the path of a flock, or grain laced with strychnine might be scattered near the sheep's bed ground at night so the hungry sheep would eat it as they moved out in the morning.

When a stubborn sheepman insisted on his own rights to the public domain, he might receive a visit from an impromptu posse of cowboys. They usually outnumbered the herders by at least 4 to 1, if only because cattle tending took that much more man power. To avoid being recognized, the visitors would cover their faces, often using old cloth sacks with eyeholes and thus giving rise to the term by which sheepmen knew them: gunnysackers. Most often these unwelcome guests would whoop down on a sheep camp under cover of night, while the herder was asleep in his tent or wagon. They were usually content to empty their revolvers at his pots and pans, scatter his flock and ride off into the darkness before the hapless sheepman could manage a riposte.

On one occasion cowhands working for a large Arizona ranch came upon two herders peacefully cooking breakfast and ordered them to break camp on

119

ing them in every direction. An ingenious variation on this was employed by some cattlemen north of Flagstaff, Arizona, in 1884. Ten flocks being trailed together from New Mexico—25,000 sheep in all—had just settled down on their bed grounds when a hundred wild mustangs burst from some nearby timberland and stampeded straight for them. From the tail of each horse swung a lash of dry rawhide, and many had cowbells clanging around their necks to goad them to greater speeds. A band of cowboys rode in their wake, yelling wildly and firing their guns. The surprised herders tried to fend off the attack with rifle fire, but this set the already maddened horses milling among the terrified sheep. Hundreds of sheep were killed, and it took a week for the herders to regroup the rest of the flocks.

The most devastating attacks were those that exploited the sheep's own flocking instinct and made them destroy themselves. Shouting, shooting raiders had only to start a flock moving toward some nearby natural hazard; the panicked sheep would push the animals in front to annihilation and then follow mindlessly along. Sometimes quicksand was the fatal trap. Four thousand head were driven to their deaths in the bottomless sands under the Little Colorado River in eastern Arizona in 1884.

More often the sheep were driven over cliffs, a technique known as rim-rocking. Perfected by the Plains Indians in their buffalo hunts, rim-rocking was particularly well adapted to the mountain pastures where sheep often grazed. In one instance 3,800 were stampeded over a bluff into a stream ironically named Parachute Creek near the town of Rifle, Colorado. The next day residents found pieces of paper scattered in the streets bearing the cattlemen's admonition, "Mum's the word."

Reputable cattlemen and their associations publicly repudiated the sheep raids and sometimes offered rewards for the capture of particularly vicious raiders. But in cattle country no one was ever arrested for running sheep off the government-owned range, and seldom was anyone convicted of slaughtering sheep. When herders as well as sheep were killed, the law usually took some notice, but not always with great effect. In southeastern Arizona in 1889 three Mexican herders were shot dead and another wounded by

the spot. The riders then roared with delight as the herders tried to strap their red hot camp stove to the back of an unwilling pack animal.

As grass ran out and tempers grew short, such bullying gave way to uglier means of intimidation. Teams of club-wielding cowboys (the clubs were usually spokes taken from the wheels of a sheep wagon) would ride through bleating, helpless flocks, smashing skulls until they grew arm-weary. Or they might stand back and pick off sheep one by one with rifles. But such methods were time-consuming. Resourceful cowhands turned to dynamite charges fitted with percussion caps. In a tightly bunched flock a few accurately thrown sticks could kill or maim dozens of sheep. Fire was even more diabolically efficient. The frightened animals instinctively huddled together, and one or two woollies ignited in a closed corral would soon touch off the whole flock. One night in 1887 a sheepman lost 2,600 head to the torch in his pens near Tie Siding, Wyoming.

Another terror tactic was to stampede a herd of cattle through a band of sheep, trampling and scatter-

Ranch manager James Bower, photographed with his wife, Sarah, was a silent witness to the murders for which Diamondfield Jack was wrongly convicted. Bower later named the real killer—just in time to save Jack from the hangman.

three cowboys who had just finished sharing breakfast with them. In reporting the story the Tombstone *Daily Prospector* editorialized cautiously: "We are perfectly aware that it is exceedingly annoying and vexatious to cattlemen to have sheep run on their ranges; but we do not think the provocation great enough to justify wholesale murder." At the trial six months later, the accused put forward an implausible tale of self-defense—and were set free.

In regions where flocks were long established and prejudice was not an issue, public sentiment sometimes swung in favor of the victimized sheepmen, and in one celebrated instance justice appears to have miscarried *against* the cattle interests, in the person of a boastful cowboy bully called Diamondfield Jack.

During the summer of 1895, Jackson Lee Davis hired on with the enormous Sparks-Harrell Cattle Company in southern Idaho. His nickname, Diamondfield, had been given to him several years earlier by a fellow cowpuncher because of Davis' repeated allusions to his brief career as a diamond prospector near Silver City. He also had the reputation of being a ready hand with a gun.

John Sparks paid Davis top money—$50 a week—to work as an "outside man" patrolling the deadline that ran north and south through the middle of Cassia County. Davis was to see to it that the increasingly restive sheepmen crowded into the eastern end of the county did not move their animals across the line into cattle country. "Keep the sheep back," Davis was instructed. "Don't kill, but shoot to wound if necessary. If you do have to kill, the company will stand behind you."

Davis went about his new job with relish, accosting sheepmen along the deadline, waving his gun and threatening dire consequences if they failed to keep to their side. In November he wounded a herder who had confronted him with a rifle, but apparently out of contrition he carried the man back to his sheep camp. A few months later, riding at night, he came upon a sheep camp and fired a dozen shots in its general direction. Sheepmen returned the fire, and Davis rode off. The only casualty was a horse in the camp.

Three days after this incident Davis left the ranch where he had been staying and headed south toward Wells, Nevada, stopping en route at some of the half a dozen Sparks-Harrell ranches in the region. In the bars and brothels of Wells he boasted that he had been in a shooting scrape in Idaho, and as he drifted through other towns and ranches in Nevada he continued to talk.

Meanwhile, in Cassia County two young sheepherders had been discovered shot to death in their wagon. Their bodies were badly decomposed, and their sheep dogs, tied to the wagon wheels, were nearly dead of starvation. The dead men had last been seen alive by a fellow herder 12 days before their bodies were found, the same day that Diamondfield Jack had left for Nevada.

News of the murders, and of Davis' boastful talk, spread quickly, and a connection between the two was readily drawn by embittered sheepmen. In a matter of weeks Davis was charged with the murders; local woolgrowers' associations helped put up a $4,600 reward for his capture. Thanks to a tip from a disaffected former Sparks-Harrell ranch hand named Frank Smith, who knew that one of his old colleagues was getting letters from the suspect, Davis was traced to Yuma, Arizona, where he was serving time under an alias for "aggravated battery" against a peace officer. In March 1897 Davis was taken back to Cassia County to stand trial for the murders.

Cattle baron John Sparks made good on his promise that the company would back up Davis if he had to kill. Sparks hired three lawyers to defend Davis, among them James H. Hawley of Boise, one of the most skilled courtroom attorneys in the West. But the sheepmen were not going to be outdone; in support of the county prosecutor, they (and, it was said, the Mormon Church, since both victims were Mormons) brought in another lawyer from out of state and a third from Boise. The latter was William E. Borah, a future United States Senator.

Albion, the county seat where the trial took place, was deep in sheep country, and all of the jurors lived on the sheep side of the deadline, though none was himself a sheepman. The prosecution's case depended on the testimony of Frank Smith, who stood to collect the reward if Davis was convicted, and on the dubious proposition that Davis had ridden more than 50 miles in five hours on the day of the murders—

from the Idaho ranch he had left that morning to the murder site farther north and then south to the Nevada ranch where he was seen early in the afternoon. Several witnesses testified that such a ride would have taken at least 10 hours, but the jury was unconvinced. Diamondfield Jack was pronounced guilty of murder and sentenced to hang.

Defense attorney Hawley began a series of court appeals and petitions to Idaho's Board of Pardons that grew more desperate as the day appointed for Davis' hanging approached. Then, with the execution just over a week away, the pardon board received a remarkable deposition. James E. Bower, superintendent of all the Sparks-Harrell ranches, swore that he had been present at the killings and that the fatal shots had been fired by Jeff Gray, a local cowhand he had been riding with. They had joined the sheepherders in their wagon at lunchtime, Bower wrote, and an argument developed over range rights. When one of the herders attacked Bower, Gray jumped from the wagon and fired in self-defense. Bower added that neither he nor Gray thought the herders were badly hurt. He expected that they would soon contact their fellow herders and that he and Gray "would be pursued and mobbed." According to the deposition, Diamondfield Jack had nothing to do with the incident, but Bower had been so confident that an innocent man would not be punished that he had waited until Davis was all but mounting the gallows before coming forward.

Jeff Gray signed an affidavit confirming Bower's story in detail, and several cattlemen swore Bower or Gray had told them the same story shortly after the killings. Davis and his lawyers were jubilant. Surely the pardon board could not ignore such conclusive evidence of his innocence. But the prosecutors suspected that collusion was involved in the confessions, and the pardon board was still subjected to steady pressure from sheepmen and possibly from the Mormons who were held to believe in "blood atonement." Regardless of his guilt or innocence of the killings in question, some felt Davis had "done enough and ought to be hanged on general principles."

Diamondfield Jack's pardon was denied, and only a last-minute stay from the U.S. Court of Appeals in San Francisco spared him from the hangman. Bower and Gray were tried for the killings and acquitted on grounds of self-defense, but Davis remained in jail under sentence of death. Hawley sent further petitions to the pardon board. Gradually, public opinion began to shift in Davis' favor. Two of the prosecutors at his trial wrote to the board that they now believed him to be innocent. "It seems incredible," said one, "that two men, in order to save the life of a man apparently as worthless as Jack Davis, would confess to the taking of human lives."

Still the pardon board dithered. After another last-minute stay had taken Davis from the gallows, they commuted his sentence to life imprisonment. Finally, in December 1902, after more than five years in Idaho jails, Davis was granted a full pardon.

By the end of the Diamondfield Jack affair, the passionate antagonism of sheepmen and cattlemen in southern Idaho appeared to have spent itself, and the two interests reached a grudging accommodation. But 300 miles to the east in Wyoming, still a stronghold of big-time cattlemen, the war on the woollybacks was just entering its final and most virulent stage. Hostilities were to last another seven years, until a brutal triple murder so repelled the public that the worst of the butchery stopped.

On the night of April 3, 1909, sheep owners Joseph Allemand and Joseph Emge, along with a young French herder, Jules Lazair, were asleep in their wagon on the north side of Spring Creek, not far from the little settlement of Tensleep in the Bighorn basin. On the south side of the creek in another wagon slept two more herders, a Frenchman named Pierre Cafferal and a boy, Charles Helmer, who was known as Bounce.

Allemand was a well-established sheepman, popular even among the local cattle owners. Emge had recently switched his business from cattle to sheep, and if he was not beloved of his former colleagues, he had no reason to expect trouble, particularly since he and his partner were camped on the acknowledged range of a fellow sheepman. To get there, however, they had ignored warnings to drive their flock around a large cattle range and had gone through it instead, across a well-known deadline.

Shortly after the herders had gone to sleep, a gang of masked raiders stormed the wagon on the south side of the creek, hauled Cafferal and young Helmer out of bed and put them under guard. The remaining attackers then closed in on the other wagon and riddled it with bullets, killing Emge and Lazair inside. As the raiders piled sagebrush against the side of the wagon to burn it, Allemand stumbled out, apparently wounded. One of the gunnysackers ordered him to throw up his hands, which he did. Whereupon another shouted, "This is a hell of a time of night to come out here with your hands up!" and shot him dead. The marauders finished up by setting fire to both of the wagons and shooting a couple of dozen sheep and several dogs.

The raiders had providently severed nearby telephone wires, so information about the killings was slow in getting to Basin, the county seat, and the sheriff and county prosecutor did not reach Spring Creek until late the next afternoon. "The sight that greeted them," reported the *Thermopolis Record,* "was almost too horrible for belief. The bodies lay where they fell, those of Emge and Lazair in the charred ruins of the wagon, burned almost beyond recognition." Beside the wagon, lying on Allemand's body and curled up next to it, were two small furry pups, the only surviving sheep dogs.

A light snow had fallen, which had obliterated most of the telltale tracks of the raiders, but the sheriff spotted the imprint of a half-soled boot with the heel worn down on one side. The bodies were removed to a ranch house located nearby, and a few local hands arrived to have a look. As they were leaving, the sheriff noticed that one of them, a cowboy named Herbert Brink, was wearing a boot with a half sole and a worn-down heel.

Within three weeks lawmen had arrested Brink and an excattleman named Ed Eaton, whom Bounce Helmer had recognized during the raid. Before the month was out, a grand jury had been convened and more than 50 witnesses had been subpoenaed. Rewards of $5,500 had been offered for information that would lead to the arrest and the conviction of the murderers, the majority of it put up by the state and county woolgrowers' associations. Sheepmen were in the process of raising an additional $20,000 to aid the prosecution when one of the subpoenaed witnesses committed suicide, leaving behind a note that incriminated a couple of well-known local cattlemen.

Early in May indictments for murder and arson were handed down against seven men: Herbert Brink, Ed Eaton, Thomas Dixon, William Keyes, Charles Farris, George Sabin and Milton Alexander. Sabin and Alexander were described by the *Thermopolis Record* as "particularly prominent."

A week later Keyes and Farris confessed to their part in the attack and agreed to turn state's evidence. They had apparently been coerced into joining the raid and had been told that nothing but sheep would be killed. Keyes and Farris were quickly separated from their codefendants and hustled off to Sheridan for their own protection. Basin, where the trial was to be held, was bristling with weapons and hostility. Sheepmen and cattlemen were encamped at opposite ends of the town issuing threats at each other as well as at sheriff's deputies and potential jurors. The Wyoming National Guard had to be called in to keep the peace until trial time in November.

Impartial jurors were brought in from the far side of the Bighorn basin, and Farris and Keyes were escorted back from Sheridan to testify. Farris identified Brink as the man who had fired the fatal shot at the surrendering Allemand. He was found guilty of first-degree murder and sentenced to hang. The remaining four defendants then quickly entered guilty pleas, Sabin and Alexander to second-degree murder, and Eaton and Dixon to arson. Brink's sentence was commuted to life imprisonment, and the others' sentences ranged between three and 26 years.

There was some grousing among sheep partisans over a supposed deal the cattlemen had made to save their necks, particularly after a few of them got early paroles. Nevertheless, the rights of sheepmen had been affirmed and that was an encouraging sign. Although isolated skirmishes occurred for another decade, the Tensleep murders proved to be the last real battle of the sheepman-cattleman wars.

Ironically, the same conditions that precipitated the violent range wars on the High Plains eventually brought peace and stability. Millions of acres had been heedlessly overstocked and overgrazed, and the crowding sparked conflicts. But problems engendered by overuse would not go away; they had to be faced,

Raids on sheep camps seldom made news, but when respected sheepmen were murdered near Tensleep, Wyoming, in 1909 the *Thermopolis Record* put the story on page one. The resulting outcry helped end the state's sheepman-cattleman wars.

THE FUTURE COUNTY SEAT OF HOT SPRINGS COUNTY.

Assassins Raid Camp

One of the Bloodiest Affairs in Many Years in the Range History of Wyoming

THREE MEN KILLED AT NIGHT

ARMED MOB LEAVES AWFUL TRAIL OF DESOLATION AND DEATH

Another tragedy of the range has been enacted, and more blood marks the trail of "civilization."

Last Friday night a band of fifteen or twenty armed men attacked the sheep camp of Joe Allemand and Joe Emge on Spring creek, a small stream that empties into Nowood above Tensleep. Allemand, Emge and a herder named Lazair were sleeping in a wagon on a high point on one side of the creek and two of the herders were in a wagon on the other side. The latter two were taken captive first and were marched a few hundred yards away, where they were held under guard until the tragedy was over and then ordered to move on and not look back. The wires had been cut so that no word was received at Basin until next day.

After taking the two herders captive the mob opened fire on the wagon in which the other men were sleeping. Allemand got out but was found a short distance away with a bullet hole in his left side and one in his neck. The wagon was riddled with holes and Emge and Lazair were probably killed at the first volley. When the mob was satisfied the men were dead they approached the wagon and set it on fire, first saturating it with coal oil. The other wagon was also burned, as well as a supply wagon and a buckboard, and several sheep dogs and about twenty-five head of sheep were killed.

Sheriff Alston and a deputy and County Attorney Metz went to the scene of the assassination immediately on receipt of the news. The sight that greeted them was almost too horrible for belief. The bodies lay where they fell, those of Emge and Lazair in the charred ruins of the wagon, burned almost beyond recognition. An automatic revolver and rifle lay under Emge's body and a rifle on top of the body of Lazair. Near the creek was a stone on which was a bunch of bloody black hair and little pools of blood were near at hand, which leads to the belief that at least one of the raiders was wounded, and this may lead to their discovery.

There was a sensational report yesterday morning that the sheriff and a deputy had been killed by the raiders, but this was wholly unfounded. The officers are not making public what they find in the way of incriminating evidence. $2,500 reward has been offered for the conviction of the assassins, and it is thought the state will add considerable more.

Allemand and Emge were both old timers in the basin and both were highly respected. Allemand has been in the sheep business for many years, while Emge had recently sold his cattle and bought sheep. Lazair was a citizen of France, and this may put an international aspect on the affair and cause the United States to take a hand in bringing the perpetrators of the outrage to justice.

A large delegation of Masons from Basin, where Allemand held membership in the order, went up to Spring creek and held ritualistic services over his remains.

GRAND OPENING

The grand op___ ___ll of the Washak___

WEATHER REPORT

Following is the weath__ ___rt of Therm___

and in time this forced fundamental changes in the way the range was used.

The beef bonanza of the 1880s had made grass so precious that ranchers were scrambling to grab title to as much land as they could in order to exclude their neighbors. When barbed wire became widely available early in the decade, stockmen took to fencing their water holes and streams, and before long they had strung wire around great expanses of public range—which, legal sanctions notwithstanding, they regarded as their own. Often they completely enclosed homesteads and small ranches, cutting off their accustomed grass and water, and a few arrogant cattle kings even encircled whole towns. A series of fence-cutting wars ensued almost as bitter as the sheepman-cattleman conflicts. In 1885 a federal law prohibited the fencing of public land, and President Grover Cleveland ordered all illegal fences cut; he authorized the Army to do the job if no one else would.

But it was nature, not the Army, that settled the issue: the Die-Up in the winter of 1886-1887 made fencing disputes moot. Prices plunged as bankrupt ranchers scrambled to sell out, and the once-abundant investment capital went elsewhere. To some ruined cattlemen, even sheep began to look attractive. Sheep had withstood the cold with fewer losses, and they fared better on a depleted range because of their ability to browse on scanty vegetation. Soon it was not uncommon for a cattleman to start running a few woollies "just to make out."

Gradually, more of the public range found its way into private hands. Railroads were granted government land, which they could sell or lease to defray construction expenses. States, too, were granted up to a million irrigable acres to develop and sell to settlers. Old homestead claims that had not been "proved up" were sold off by banks, while new homesteaders, nothing daunted, were pushing into the arid plains, using advanced techniques and equipment to raise crops with meager rainfall.

A rancher with land of his own would now string legal fences around his spread, dig irrigation ditches and wells, put up windmills to pump water, raise fodder crops for winter feed and in general run a stock farm rather than a ranch. Cowboys became farm hands—though they would have bridled at the

term—and roaming sheepherders began to disappear, for the sheep were simply put out to pasture like cattle. And to the cattlemen's surprise, when sheep were sensibly handled they actually improved the grasslands. Left to themselves, they scattered, instead of clustering in the tight bunch that was so convenient for the herder but so destructive to the grass. If they were not overstocked and were afforded well-spaced water holes, no part of the range would become "sheeped." Their hooves harrowed the soil rather than trampling it, and their droppings proved to be a valuable fertilizer.

Moreover, cattle and sheep could share the same range land. Cattle did not show any revulsion at the smell a scattered flock left behind on the grass and actually seemed to prefer the rich, rank grass of sheep's old bed-grounds.

Nevertheless, cattlemen clung to their misconceptions about sheep, especially that they drank more water than cattle and left the ground poisoned for steers that followed them. Both notions were neatly disproved by a certain sheepman who arrived with his flocks to take up ranching in cattle country by the Pecos River. According to the tale, hostile cattlemen greeted him there. "This range ain't no good for sheep," the cattlemen told him. "There's not enough water. Your sheep'll shorely die." The sheepman looked at the thriving cattle nearby and said it looked as though they were doing pretty well.

"Oh, yeah," replied the cattlemen. "But sheep's different. Sheep need more water'n cows. You shorely know that?"

Knowing that sheep really needed less water than cattle, the sheepman brought in his flocks. Soon there was a drought; the cattlemen's water holes went dry, but the sheepman and his abstemious animals had plenty of water left. The cattlemen, desperate to save their animals, had no choice but to drive them to the sheepman's ranch. When they got there the sheepman was waiting with a look of mock concern on his face.

"Good Lord, men," the sheepman said, "don't you know that these sheep have poisoned the range? Your cattle are bound to die if you bring 'em on it. You shorely know that?"

The cattlemen replied with what can only be called sheepish grins and led the animals to water. ◉

The wire that fenced the West

For decades many Western ranchers and farmers sought a means of fencing their stock and crops in and everybody else out. The rock and wooden fences of the East were too expensive on the Plains, which had few boulders and fewer trees. Plain wire fences failed to hold up against a thundering herd. For a time farmers tried thorn hedges, but the hedges required years to grow.

It took a canny Illinois farmer, Joseph F. Glidden *(right),* to combine the concepts of smooth wire and prickly hedges and devise the first practical barbed wire in 1874. Within a decade 120 million pounds a year were being sold, and the open range was changing to enclosed pasture and farmland.

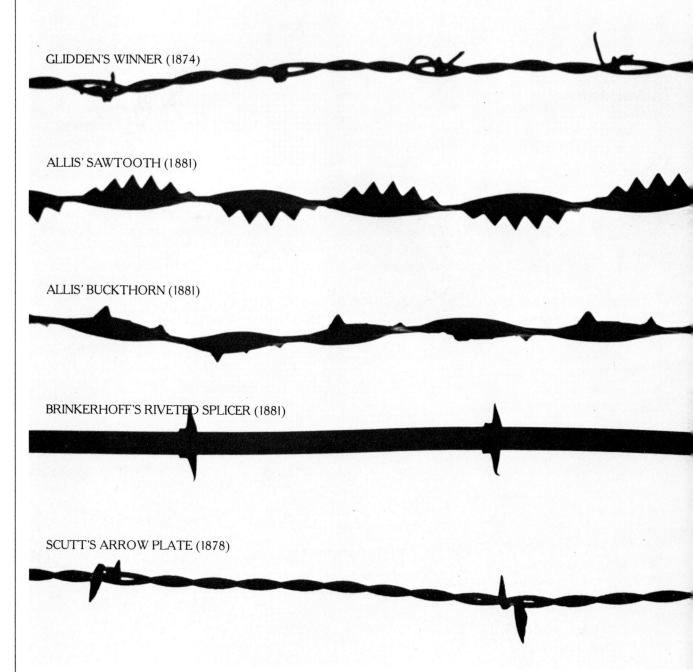

GLIDDEN'S WINNER (1874)

ALLIS' SAWTOOTH (1881)

ALLIS' BUCKTHORN (1881)

BRINKERHOFF'S RIVETED SPLICER (1881)

SCUTT'S ARROW PLATE (1878)

Anxious to share the barbed-wire bonanza, inventors patented nearly a thousand designs between 1874 and 1892. Five popular types

In later life Joseph Glidden looked every inch the tycoon, but he was merely a prosperous farmer in 1874 when he took out a barbed-wire patent. He got the idea from a crude prototype he saw at a fair and barely beat an Illinois neighbor to the draw.

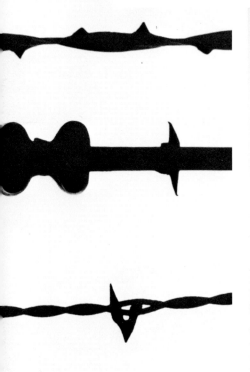

The original working model of Glidden's barbing machine was an old-fashioned coffee mill with its casing cut away and its grinder altered to cut and coil small lengths of wire. The barbs were strung by hand between strands of plain wire.

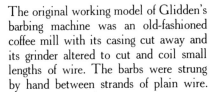

are silhouetted above at half the actual size.

GLIDDEN PATENT STEEL BARBED WIRE POSSESSES THESE CLAIMS:

It is the strongest, cheapest and most durable of fence materials, as will appear from the universal testimony of those who have used it, as well as from the facts we are to present in the following pages.

The three leading kinds of Barbed Wire are the

Glidden Patent Two Point Barbed Wire.
Glidden Patent Thickset Barbed Wire.
Glidden Patent Four Point Barbed Wire.

The Glidden Patent Two Point has for several reasons led the market as the best and most popular Barbed Wire known from its Strength, Lightness, adaptability to all uses in Fencing and its imperishable character when once in place.

The Glidden Patent Thickset is an advanced form of last named in which increased protection is furnished by barbs more closely set. It is in great favor with all who have used it. It will turn hogs. Especially adapted to sheep husbandry as a protection against dogs.

The Glidden Patent Four Point has been rapidly adopted by very many who see great advantage in the increased number of points presented in the barbs.

In each of these the Glidden principle is preserved one and the same; a sharply pricking barb strongly attached to one of the wires of the fence strand, upon which the other wire is strongly twisted, holding the barb firmly in place. The barb is at right angles to the wire and does not form a hook but a straight, **short, sharp steel thorn.**

In an advertising poster distributed around 1880, animals both wild and domestic sail easily over circus barriers but come to a screeching halt in front of Glidden's barbed wire. The brochure above extols the merits of three of Glidden's advanced designs. Unfortunately, when the wire first came into use it was all too effective; cattle and horses that ran into it were often maimed beyond saving. Ranchers resorted to wire cutting and even more violent steps to protect their stock. Eventually, the animals learned to fear all barriers. As one cowboy recalled, "You could hardly drive them between two posts."

For all its savage cruelty, the violence that broke out so frequently on the open range was usually impersonal—coldly deliberate action taken in defense of property. It did not generally matter whether the antagonists knew each other; it was what they were, not who they were, that was the reason for the conflict. But if personal or family feelings did get mixed up in a range dispute, the violence turned even more vicious and implacable.

So it was with Arizona's Pleasant Valley War, which for the ferocious tenacity of its combatants was unmatched in the annals of the West. It began during the beef bonanza of the 1880s in a remote valley northeast of Phoenix that had attracted a band of organized rustlers. As cattle and horses disappeared, ranchers began to suspect and then accuse one another of stealing them. Charges and recriminations escalated to killing, and before the shooting stopped more than five years later at least 25 people, perhaps as many as 50, were dead; the bloodletting had become so frenzied that the exact toll was never known.

Underlying the hostilities was an eye-for-an-eye vendetta between two families, the Grahams and the Tewksburys. Of seven brothers on both sides, only one survived the war.

Spread beneath the 7,000-foot height of the Mogollon Rim in a secluded corner of Apache country, Pleasant Valley in the 1870s was an arduous two-day ride from the nearest town, the little mining community of Globe, and it was more than 100 miles from the territorial capital at Prescott. Still, as the Apache threat subsided toward the end of the decade, the valley's 50-mile-long oval of lush, well-watered meadows began to attract ranchers and their herds.

Among the first to come were the Tewksbury brothers, the sons of a New Englander who had sailed to California during the gold rush. There the senior Tewksbury settled, married an Indian woman and had four children. After his wife died in 1878, he and his sons followed news of silver strikes to Arizona. The next year the three eldest sons, Edwin, John and James, left their father in Globe with a new wife and their youngest brother, Frank, and moved north into Pleasant Valley and a herd of blooded horses.

Other ranchers followed, some of whom, for their own shady reasons, found the valley's remoteness a

John Tewksbury *(inset),* a victim of the Graham-Tewksbury feud, was ambushed near his family's ranch *(below).* His body was attacked by hogs while the assailants kept his brothers besieged in the cabin.

positive attraction. In 1882, while buying supplies in Globe, Ed Tewksbury met a tall young Iowan named Tom Graham who, like the Tewksburys, had been drawn to the territory by reports of silver strikes. When Graham said he and his younger brother John were looking for a place to locate a herd of cattle, Tewksbury invited him to come to Pleasant Valley. Graham accepted, and after spending a few days with the Tewksburys, he chose a site on Canyon Creek about a mile and a half north of his hosts' spread.

For a while the neighboring families were apparently on the best of terms, the Grahams tending their small herd of cattle while the Tewksburys took care of their horses. The Grahams' herd grew rapidly, so rapidly in fact that they soon needed additional cowboys to handle it. The third Graham brother, Billy, was brought in to help, and Jim Tewksbury hired on for a generous $50 a month.

In 1883 the Grahams bought 200 heifers from a rancher northwest of the valley, and Jim went along to help drive them back. Setting out for home, the Grahams announced that they planned to do a little mavericking—referring to the common practice of picking up whatever loose, unbranded stock could be found along the way. But as they left the range of the man who had sold them the heifers, one of his cowboys rode up to collect any strays that happened to have gotten mixed in with the Grahams' new herd. The Grahams helped him cut out about a dozen strays, saying they had planned to return them themselves, but as the cowhand drove the strays back onto his boss's range, two Graham men followed at a distance. When the cowhand eventually left the strays to find their own way home, the Grahams' men rounded them up and drove them back to their herd.

Jim Tewksbury returned home and reported what had happened. His father, visiting the ranch at the time, was appalled and insisted that Jim give up his job—and his badly needed wages. The senior Tewksbury ordered his sons to have nothing more to do with the Grahams. The brothers obediently and abruptly cut ties with the Grahams—thus incurring their lasting ill will and setting a fuse to the bloody explosion that followed.

Other ranchers in the area had also been losing cattle, and they had begun to suspect that the rapid growth of the Grahams' herd was not due wholly to the brothers' good fortune and expert husbandry. One of the Grahams' neighbors, James Stinson, charged them with larceny, but when the case came to trial, prosecution witnesses failed to turn up—possibly fearing reprisals—and the Grahams were acquitted.

By now, however, suspicions were widespread and tempers were short. Stinson's range foreman, a hotheaded Texan named John Gilliland, had become friendly with the Grahams and was evidently unhappy at seeing them singled out for blame; he deliberately provoked a dispute with the Tewksburys over some misbranded cattle. The quarrel reached its height when Gilliland, having stiffened his resolve with whiskey, rode with his young nephew to the Tewksbury ranch and insulted Ed, who responded in kind. Gilliland pulled a gun and took a shot at Tewksbury, who grabbed a .22-caliber rifle and fired back, wounding both Gilliland and his nephew.

The Grahams filed charges against the Tewksburys over the shooting, and Ed and his brothers were obliged to ride to Prescott through miserable January weather to appear in court. There the judge dismissed the charges, ruling that Ed had fired in self-defense and rebuking the Grahams for their capricious prosecution. But the Tewksburys' triumph was short-lived. The youngest family member, Frank, had come from Globe to attend the trial, and he accompanied his brothers back to Pleasant Valley; but there he died of pneumonia brought on by the rigors of the trip. The Tewksburys held the Grahams responsible.

Early in 1884 Mart Blevins and his five sons arrived from Texas and set up a small cattle ranch adjoining the Graham spread. The two outfits shared some grazing land, and the Blevins boys soon became active Graham partisans. One of them, Andy, was a notorious tough who had changed his name from Blevins to Cooper because he was wanted in Texas for cattle theft and in Oklahoma for selling whiskey to Indians. Cooper took to entertaining some of his old cronies from Texas who were working north of the valley as cowboys for the big Aztec Land and Cattle Company, known in the area as the Hashknife outfit after the shape of its brand.

Before long, Cooper's friends were spending more and more time hanging around the Blevins and the

Graham ranches, and it was soon apparent that the association was founded on more than simple good fellowship. Together with their hosts, the Hashknife boys were helping to expand the mavericking of a few neighbors' cattle into one of the most extensive and lucrative rustling operations in the entire Southwest, reaching out far beyond Pleasant Valley through Arizona, Utah and Colorado, and into Mexico. One rancher who lost virtually all of his livestock described the rustlers as a "thoroughly organized band of criminals" who sought "by hook or crook to take possession of the valley."

The Tewksburys' herd of fine horses was a frequent target of the rustlers, and the evidence invariably pointed to Andy Cooper, the Grahams and their friends. The Tewksburys accused the Grahams of theft; the Grahams in turn called the mixed-blood Tewksburys "Injuns" and "blacks" and vowed to "run the damn blacks out of the country."

The killing began in February 1887. The Daggs brothers of Flagstaff, owners of the largest sheep operation in northern Arizona, had been repeatedly harassed and driven from their accustomed range north of the Mogollon Rim by Hashknife raiders. In desperation they sought new winter grazing land south of the deadline that ran along the rim, in the lush pastures of Pleasant Valley where no sheepman had ventured before. The Daggs hired a Basque herder with two Indian helpers to move the main flock south. William Jacobs, an old friend of the Tewksburys, went along, driving two small bands of the Daggs's sheep that he tended on shares. According to some accounts, one or more Tewksbury partisans went along with their rifles, riding guard.

As the flock approached the Mogollon Rim, the herdsmen were ambushed. The sheep were rim-rocked over a convenient cliff, and the Basque was shot dead. His body was found beheaded, and Arizona newspapers reported that the murderers had been trailed to the Graham ranch. The other herders managed to escape by dark and sought refuge at the Tewksburys'.

There was no immediate reaction, but several months later the Grahams' friend old Mart Blevins rode out from his ranch looking for some missing horses and failed to return. His son Hampton Blevins

set out with a few Hashknife cowboys to look for him. After a few days they concluded they were unlikely to find him, and their purpose shifted to revenge; they were certain the Tewksburys were responsible. One of them remarked to a friend that they planned "to start a little old war of our own."

On August 9, Hampton Blevins and four Hashknife cowboys rode, heavily armed, up to a ranch north of the Tewksburys'. Jim and Ed Tewksbury and two of their friends were inside the cabin. From horseback the visitors shouted that they wanted to come in for something to eat. "We aren't keeping a boarding house," Jim Tewksbury yelled back, "especially for the likes of you!"

Inevitably, gunplay followed. It is not known who fired the first shot, but Hampton Blevins was the first casualty, blasted from his saddle with a bullet in his brain. John Paine, a notorious Hashknife gunman, fired back at Jim Tewksbury but in an instant his horse was hit and crashed to the ground, pinning Paine underneath. As he struggled free and ran for cover a second shot clipped one of his ears, and a third and fatal slug sent him sprawling in the dust. Another of the Hashknife cowboys was nearly knocked from his saddle by a bullet in the chest but managed to cling to his horse as it galloped away. The remaining two horsemen suffered superficial wounds. Within a little more than 10 seconds all five of the riders had been struck by gunfire from the cabin; two were dead and the rest had ridden off in a total rout. No one inside the cabin was hurt.

Eight days later the vendetta claimed its next victim, the youngest Graham, 18-year-old Billy. On his way back from a dance at the Central Hotel in Phoenix, Billy was crossing a creek a few miles from his home when he met James Houck, a deputy sheriff of Apache County and a brother-in-law of the butchered Basque sheepherder. As Houck later recounted, "We both drew at sight of one another, but I shot first and got him." Billy clung to his saddle until he reached the Graham ranch, where he died the next day.

With the killing of the youngest Graham, the feud became a struggle for vengeance to the last man. Two weeks after Billy's death, the Graham faction, which had clearly been taking a beating, set out to even things up. Early on the morning of September 2, a

The once-prosperous Graham ranch lay bleak and neglected in 1890, the third year of the bloody feud with the Tewksburys. Two of the Graham brothers had been killed, and the last of them had moved away to try to start a new life.

large party left the Graham-Blevins stronghold and rode toward the Tewksbury ranch. They arrived at sunrise and concealed themselves among the rocks and bushes on a hillside not far from the cabin. Down below, oblivious to their peril, John Tewksbury and William Jacobs were tending a few horses. Suddenly a volley of rifle fire exploded from behind the rocks. Jacobs died at once, a ragged hole ripped in his back by three well-grouped shots. Tewksbury took a single bullet in the back of the neck but he probably did not die immediately, for his body was found later with the skull crushed by a heavy stone.

The raiders closed in on the ranch headquarters, where the two remaining Tewksbury brothers, Ed

and Jim, together with their father and a friend, barricaded themselves in the thick-walled cabin and prepared for a siege. As both sides fired sporadically, the situation took an unexpected grisly turn. A band of half-wild hogs appeared just beyond rifle range and, to the horror of those inside the cabin, began to root and grunt about the bodies of their two fallen comrades, starting to make a meal of them. The Tewksburys called frantically to their assailants, but the Graham bunch refused to grant a truce for burial or even to allow someone to drive the beasts away.

When the siege was finally lifted after several days, the corpses were so mangled and bloated that burial was a nauseating task. Jim Tewksbury summed up his

The final casualty of the Pleasant Valley War, Tom Graham *(above)* was shot in 1892. At an ensuing hearing his widow, Anne *(left)*, pulled out a gun and attempted to shoot one of Tom's accused killers.

feelings later: "No damned man can kill a brother of mine and stand guard over him for the hogs to eat him, and live within a mile and a half of me."

Two days after the siege began Andy Cooper turned up 75 miles away in a saloon in the little town of Holbrook, boasting that he had killed one of the Tewksburys and another man. From the saloon he retired to a cottage just across the railroad tracks, where his brother John Blevins had installed their widowed mother not long before. Word of Cooper's arrival and of his boasts soon reached the newly elected sheriff of Apache County, Commodore Perry Owens (whose parents, it seemed, had admired the hero of the Battle of Lake Erie). Owens had been under pressure from local cattlemen to do something about the area's rampaging rustlers, and Andy Cooper was reputed to be the worst of the bunch. The sheriff rode to Holbrook and prepared to arrest Cooper.

Once in town, Owens checked over his firearms and walked to the Blevins house. At 4:30 in the afternoon he stepped onto the porch and knocked on the door. What happened next was recounted by Owens at the inquest that followed.

He testified that as he approached the house he saw Andy Cooper and three other men inside. Eva Blevins, John's wife, opened the door and Owens strode into the house. At this point Cooper, a six-gun in his hand, stepped from behind the door of a back room just as John Blevins, also armed, opened a door from the other side of the house. For a second Owens and Cooper eyed one another in silence, then the sheriff said, "Cooper, I want you." He said he had a warrant, and added: "You must come at once."

Owens fired first, and Cooper went down with a bullet in his midsection. John Blevins fired from the other side of the room but missed, and Owens spun around and fired his Winchester from the hip, putting John out of action with a painful shoulder wound. The sheriff then ran back into the street so he could cover both sides of the house at once. At that point Mose Roberts, a friend of Cooper's, leaped through a window with a revolver in his hand; Owens fired again and brought down Roberts with a mortal wound. Finally, the youngest Blevins brother, Sam, grabbed Cooper's pistol and ran out onto the porch.

Before he could cock and aim his weapon, Owens put his fourth bullet through Sam's heart.

Two days later the coroner's jury ended its investigation and rendered its verdict, finding that Owens had acted "in discharge of his duty," clearing him of any crime. A local newspaper noted, "Outside of a few men, a very few at that, Owens is supported by every man, woman and child in town."

Not surprisingly, the Blevins' side of the story, discounted at the time, reflects considerably less credit on Commodore Perry Owens. According to John Blevins' wife, Eva, Owens fired in cold blood on an unarmed Cooper, shot Roberts in the back as he was fleeing, also unarmed, and wounded her husband from across the street. In view of Owens' remarkable emergence from the battle unscratched, this version may have deserved more attention than it received.

The Holbrook shoot-out brought the feud's death toll to 10, and it was obvious that drastic measures were needed to stop the fighting, which threatened everyone in the area. The territorial governor ordered Sheriff William Mulvenon of Yavapai County to raise a posse large enough to sweep through Pleasant Valley and arrest every man on either side he could lay hands on. Early on the morning of September 21, 1887, Mulvenon and 25 heavily armed men rode into the valley and established themselves at Perkins' store—an old stone building originally put up as a fort against Apache raids—which happened to be within sight of the Graham ranch. Rather than sally forth to confront the Grahams in their stronghold, the sheriff sent a few men in decoy parties to ride past, to lure them into a trap he was planning. He deployed the rest of his force in ambush, hidden behind the low walls of an unfinished stone building just across from the store.

Before long two men, John Graham and Charles Blevins, rode up to the store and cautiously circled it, evidently trying to find out who and how many the strangers were. As they turned to the unfinished building across the way, standing up in their stirrups to peer over the walls, Sheriff Mulvenon walked out to face them with a double-barreled shotgun and ordered them to throw up their hands.

Graham and Blevins, however, were not accustomed to letting anyone get the drop on them. They spurred their horses and reached for their guns as Mulvenon's shotgun roared. One barrel of buckshot caught Blevins in the middle of the back, and he was dead before he hit the ground. The shotgun's other blast hit Graham's horse in the neck, but Graham himself was fatally wounded by a rifle bullet from one of the hidden posse.

Sheriff Mulvenon's elaborately planned ambush had netted him only two men out of the entire Graham outfit, and the leader of the faction, Tom, was still at large. Leaving John Graham to die, the sheriff and his posse rode against the Graham ranch, but by the time they got there Tom Graham and his fighting men were missing.

Mulvenon had less trouble cornering the Tewksburys. He had sent a messenger to notify them that once the Grahams were arrested he would be along to serve warrants and take them to Prescott. When Mulvenon and his posse rode up, they found Jim and Ed Tewksbury and five others patiently waiting. They surrendered without protest but were outraged to learn that Tom Graham was still free. Within a few days of their hearing in Prescott, the Tewksburys were out on bond and back in Pleasant Valley, at liberty to pick up the feud again.

Tom Graham, still wanted by the law, now took advantage of a lull in the action to conclude some long-standing business of a personal nature. On October 8, 1887, he turned up at the home of a Baptist minister named Melton, who lived in the Salt River settlement of Tempe, not far from Phoenix. With the Reverend Mr. Melton officiating, the 33-year-old Graham was married that day to the preacher's 17-year-old daughter, Anne.

Prudently, the newlyweds decided not to take up residence in the troubled valley; Tom turned his ranch over to another man to manage on shares and bought land near Tempe on which to start a farm. To complete the picture of a reformed, married man, four days after the wedding he walked into the sheriff's office in Phoenix and inquired if there was a warrant for his arrest. On October 16, Sheriff Mulvenon, notified by the Phoenix lawman, collected Graham and took him back to Prescott for a hearing. He was freed on $3,000 bail and ordered to appear before the grand jury on the same December day as Ed and Jim Tewksbury. All three were indicted, but when the time for the trial came, witnesses failed to appear, and after two postponements all charges were dropped.

Even before that some hitherto law-abiding citizens of Pleasant Valley decided that more direct action was needed to restore order. Under wraps of strictest secrecy, a Committee of Fifty (which actually numbered closer to 20) was formed to aid the forces of law and order—chiefly, it seems, by killing anyone who was deemed a threat to peace. Al Rose, Tom Graham's close friend and one of his side's most feared gunmen, was the committee's first victim. Arrested in Sheriff Mulvenon's sweep of the valley, Rose was later released with no charges against him, but when he returned home he found a warning that he had better leave the country immediately. Rose decided to gather together his livestock before going, and the delay cost him his life. A party of vigilantes rode up to his cabin, dragged him outside and hanged him from a nearby tree.

The violence reached its peak the following summer when a mob of 30 masked riders hanged three Graham partisans. By then lynching was so rife that one rancher recalled seeing men "hanging all up and down Cherry Creek" with "maggots dropping out of them." In their zeal the grim crusaders sometimes equated suspicion with guilt; more than one stranger passing through the valley was hastily strung up for being unable to explain his presence to the satisfaction of the committee.

The effect of the hangings on Pleasant Valley's remaining troublemakers was remarkable. "No amount of shooting could terrorize the cowboy element as this lynching did," recalled one observer years later. "Some who were known to be stealing were sent word *to go* and they did *go;* some of them in a hurry. Ed Rogers, the range foreman of the Aztec Land and Cattle Company, was in such a hurry that he took the train east and sent back word to some of his friends to send his horse to him."

Not even the merciless sweep of the vigilantes, however, could extinguish the smouldering embers of the Graham-Tewksbury feud. For three years Tom Graham lived peacefully on his modest ranch near

Sole survivor Ed Tewksbury became the title character of Zane Grey's novel *To the Last Man,* a romanticized account of the Graham-Tewksbury feud. He later served undramatically as a peace officer.

Tempe. Then on August 2, 1892, while hauling a load of grain into town, he was shot to death—the final victim (as it turned out) of the violence that had begun five years before.

According to the eyewitness account of a 12-year-old boy named Ed Cummings, he and his sister Molly and another child were following a shortcut through the woods that morning when they spied two horsemen hiding in a thicket beside the road. Both men, said the boy, had their guns raised in the direction of Tom Graham, who was driving past in his four-horse team and wagon. Ed Cummings identified one of them in court as Ed Tewksbury, who lowered his gun the moment he saw the children and tried to restrain his companion. The other man, John Rhodes, pulled his trigger, however, and Graham toppled into the back of the wagon. The team of horses, startled by the gunshot, bolted down the road to the Cummings' house, where the last of the Graham brothers died a few hours later.

An alarm went out immediately, and Rhodes was tracked down and taken prisoner after a 10-mile chase. Tewksbury surrendered later at a ranch in Pleasant Valley where he was working, but he proclaimed his innocence. In order to avoid the threat of lynching, Tewksbury was smuggled into Phoenix with elaborate precautions.

Rhodes's preliminary hearing, which lasted for 10 days, produced one final piece of melodrama. As the children finished testifying that Rhodes had fired the fatal shot, Anne Graham removed her dead husband's heavy .44-caliber revolver from her handbag, pointed the gun at the nearby Rhodes and pulled the trigger. The hammer hit with a loud click. The gun had failed to fire. For an instant the courtroom was frozen, then it erupted with the screams of women as Anne Graham became hysterical and men surrounded the defendant and his assailant. Before she could do anything else, the widow's friends grabbed her by the arms

and rushed her from the room.

The hearing resumed a short time later. Rhodes produced an alibi for the time of the killing, which convinced the justice of the peace who was hearing the evidence that the prosecution had no case; he let the prisoner go. Few other citizens of Phoenix agreed; in a burst of public anger a mass meeting of townspeople condemned the justice for taking the powers of a higher bench and jury into his own inadequate hands and recommended further prosecution. But nothing came of it. John Rhodes was a free man.

Ed Tewksbury, on the other hand, was indicted and went before a jury, which deliberated for two days and found him guilty. His lawyers appealed on legal technicalities and won him a second trial; this time the jury could not agree on a verdict and was dismissed. By the time he was finally released on bail in February 1895, Ed Tewksbury had spent two and a half years in prison. A year later the prosecution, apparently believing that a conviction would now be impossible, closed the case by filing a motion to dismiss the charge.

And so, not in blazing gunfire but in a welter of inconclusive legalities, the end came to the bloodiest family feud to besmirch the history of the West. Edwin Tewksbury returned home to Pleasant Valley, but his dreams had long since gone aglimmering. His brother Jim had died of tuberculosis several years earlier, and now over the neglected family ranch ran only a few half-wild mavericks. Ed sold what little he had left and moved to the town of Globe. There, like other celebrated gunmen, he put his most well-known talent to work by becoming a law officer. His reputation, some said, was enough to make any desperado think twice before starting trouble, though the man himself was afflicted with the same disease that had killed his brother Jim. And that was what finally killed him. On April 4, 1904, the last of the feuding brothers of the Pleasant Valley War died in his bed.

Hardscrabble life on marginal ranches

A man who brought his family to ranch on the Western Plains usually had more ambition than he did money. The promise of unlimited open range land made it easy for a prospective rancher to overlook the hardships he would face in a land where water was scarce and lumber for building even scarcer.

A newly arrived rancher often spent his first year or two holed up in a lean-to or a dugout cut into a hillside near a creek. If he was fortunate enough not to have his dugout swept away by spring floods, there was always the chance he would wake up some morning to see the legs of one of his way-

ward cows sticking through the roof.

As a rancher began to reap his first profits, he built a ranch house and corrals. Even then the housing was not much: the deeper into the prairies he went, the harder it was to find straight trees to use for logs. In the absence of usable wood, the only available alter-

native was a sod house, or "soddy."

Most frontier dwellings had a sod roof. Any gaps were filled with clay, if available, or cow manure. If it rained enough, the roof could turn into a garden. One Eastern bride traveling with her husband to their Montana ranch in the early 1880s recalled that they "kept passing low, cheerless-looking log shacks, mud-daubed, with weeds sticking up out of dirt roofs." Her heart sank lower as they rode along. Finally, she asked: "Is ours as bad as that?" "Worse," her husband replied.

Fleas and bedbugs were the constant companions of every ranch family, and mice were prevalent everywhere—that is, unless the bull snakes ate them. Many ranchers persevered but others gave up, confirming the warning of a woman rancher in Wyoming, Elinore Stewart, that "persons afraid of coyotes and work and loneliness had better let ranching alone."

The families of the Tidwell brothers, Frank and Hyrum, shared a two-room log cabin on their horse and cattle ranch at Sunnyside, Utah, in the 1890s. To relieve the crowding, most of the men slept outdoors in lean-tos (left).

143

Ephraim Finch and his wife, Sarah, flank the entrance to their sod-roofed ranch house in Nebraska. They started the ranch in 1875 with 80 head of cattle. A town named after them, Finchville, was founded on their property in 1880.

Sod-house ranchers in Custer County, Nebraska, the McGaugheys raised livestock, grain and a passel of children. In spite of the hailstorms and the grasshopper plagues, they did well enough to afford a baby carriage *(left)*.

Cattle rancher Al Wise and his family gather beside a decorative elk skull and antlers at their Callaway, Nebraska, home in 1892. Wise, also county coroner, could afford a shingled roof and a crude washing machine *(left rear)*.

149

A family named Aldridge lines the fence in front of their ranch house in Utah around 1880. Among their hardships was the gusty prairie wind. It bent and shook their two scrawny trees, and often it piled dust on their meager crops.

5 | Bluebloods and big money in the Badlands

In the 1870s wealthy Easterners and Europeans began trickling west, lured into the booming cattle business by the chance for windfall profits and a vigorous, exciting life. Setting up grandiose ranches, they promptly riled their Western neighbors with beginners' mistakes and alien customs (riding on hunts in scarlet jackets). And their enthusiasm was positively overbearing.

One avid young newcomer sent home such lengthy reports that his financier father wrote back snappishly, "I do not need to know every time one of our cattle switches his tail."

By 1880 dilettantes of every sort were pouring into ranch lands throughout the West. Three barbed-wire magnates—Joseph Glidden, Isaac Elwood and Henry Sanborn followed their

prickly product from Illinois into west Texas. George Bird Grinnell, the famous authority on Indian cultures, opted for a ranch in Wyoming. But the two most famous dudes set up their spreads in an unlikely region of striped hills, deep gorges and towering mesas: the Dakota Badlands. They were New Yorker Teddy Roosevelt and the Marquis de Morès, a Frenchman.

The town of Medora, founded by the Marquis de Morès, huddles in a rugged valley in the Badlands. Morès owned most of the town, including a railroad spur across the Little Missouri River *(left rear),* a meat-packing plant *(center rear)* and a guesthouse for his in-laws *(foreground).*

THE
BEEF BONANZA

OR
HOW TO GET RICH
ON
THE PLAINS

BY
GEN. JAMES S. BRISBIN
U.S.A.

The adventures of tireless Teddy and a French marquis

Brasswork agleam and smokestack chuffing, the Northern Pacific Railroad's *Pacific Express* eased to a halt one evening in the early spring of 1883 at a whistle stop called Little Missouri on the west bank of a sluggish stream of the same name in the spectacular Dakota Badlands. The conductor jumped down to put a stepping stool on what passed for a station platform, and the trainman heaved a mountainous pile of suitcases and steamer trunks onto a waiting four-wheeled cart. Then the train's principal passenger alighted slowly, looking about at the fly-blown cluster of shacks that composed the town—"Little Misery," as its people called it.

There was a general store, a boardinghouse, a dingy hotel called the Pyramid Park and a saloon with a sign that proclaimed "Big-Mouthed Bob's Bug-Juice Dispensary." Behind these on the sagebrush flats was a cluster of gray Army barracks, originally thrown together for soldiers stationed there to protect workmen from Indians and outlaws while the railroad was being built but now were abandoned and dilapidated. The passenger, warned about the fleabags that passed for hotels on this fringe of civilization, motioned to his companion, a faithful valet and private secretary, who had checked most of their baggage in the station shack. The two men then shouldered a tent they had brought with them, walked across the railroad bridge to the east bank of the river and made camp. That night, man and manservant christened the spot with a bottle of fine wine.

The passenger was a Frenchman with a name as long as a king's—Antoine-Amédée-Marie-Vincent-Amat Manca de Vallombrosa, the Marquis de Morès et Montemaggiore—and a regal disposition to match. William F. Van Driesche, the valet, had served the Marquis de Morès for most of the nobleman's 24 years. They had come West because Morès had grown bored with life among the French aristocracy and had decided to join the ranks of America's new capitalist elite. To that end, he planned to build a commercial empire by cattle ranching and meat packing on a mammoth scale. Here, in Little Missouri, he would begin—as soon as the sun rose the next day.

Here, too, later in the year, another well-finished young man arrived on the same train, eventually to commence ranching. His name was Theodore Roosevelt, he too was 24, and he had projected himself into life with much the same attitude as the Marquis but a more sociable disposition. Morès' motto was: "Work conquers all." Roosevelt favored: "Go at it diligently, and don't fool around." Over the next four years, as the Marquis fought to win a fortune and succeeded only in losing one, the two men—both of them flamboyant, outspoken and supremely self-confident—would occasionally dine together, occasionally have their tiffs and once would almost come to a duel. Roosevelt would make no fortune either but, far more important, he would broaden his Eastern-based education with an understanding of the West and its people that would shape his dynamic career. In the end, they would part from one another, as well as with the Badlands, leaving behind a legendary tale of the two unlikeliest ranchers, and the two most audacious dudes, ever to take up with cows.

On the morning of April 2, 1883, the Marquis de Morès and his valet awoke, rented horses at the town's livery stable and set out to explore the Little Missouri Valley. To his new neighbors, this figure of

This 1881 bestseller, written by a soldier who served on the frontier but knew little about cattle, lured many a dude westward with its roseate account of ranching.

155

MORNING AT THE RANCH

Innocents from abroad

The English gentlemen in these 1880 illustrations, with their painfully stiff collars, monocles and pince-nez eyeglasses, are not untypical of the refined and often titled Europeans who flocked West during the Gilded Age, looking for wealth and a jolly good time as ranchers.

The naïveté of some of the genteel newcomers was legendary. One young Briton arrived on a Texas ranch with his luggage full of fancy sheets, dresser scarves and antimacassars. Another, having heard of Western lawlessness, brought along a small arsenal of weapons but limited his wardrobe to one spare neckerchief and a single change of socks.

Some of these foreign visitors prospered. But the inability to adapt to a new land and its rugged ways cost many an "aristocratic exploiter" both his capital and his morale.

In one Western saloon two elegant visitors were discussing the outcome of a recent Cambridge University boat race when they noticed that a broken-down bum nearby was weeping aloud. "What is it to you?" asked the gentlemen. The derelict replied, "I once stroked that crew."

SUPPER WITH THE HERDER

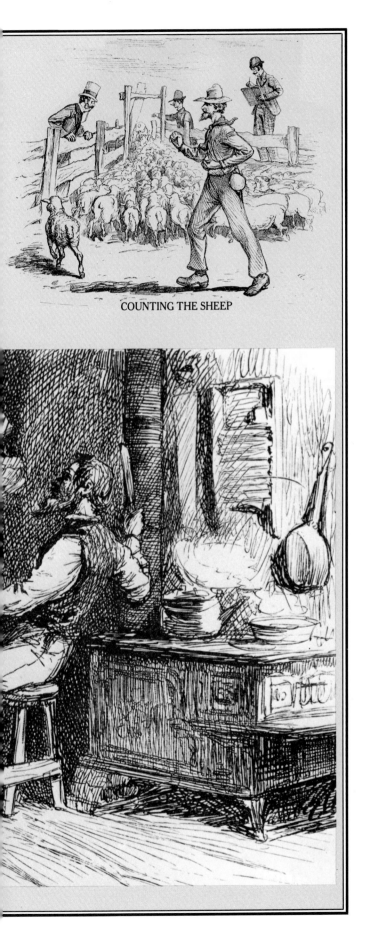

COUNTING THE SHEEP

Old World erudition appeared incomprehensibly out of place, and they immediately began calling him "the crazy Frenchman." One even went so far as to ask: "What in the world are you doing out here when all the pleasures of Paris are at your command?"

"I am tired of them all," replied the Marquis. "I am weary of civilization; I long for the wilderness; I want an absolute contrast to the old life."

It is doubtful that Morès bothered to describe his "old life," just as it is doubtful that his neighbors could have fathomed it if he had. He had been born in Paris' fashionable *faubourg* Saint-Germain, a child of proud and illustrious French and Spanish ancestry. In Paris and in a family villa on the Riviera, he was reared by governesses and a tutor from whom he learned early on to be articulate in his native tongue and fluent in English, German and Italian. After compiling impressive records at two Catholic colleges, he carried on the family military tradition by entering Saint-Cyr, the West Point of France. At Saint-Cyr and, thereafter, at the crack cavalry school of Saumur, Morès distinguished himself as a first-class rider and swordsman. But subsequent garrison duty in dull provincial towns soon palled on the intense lieutenant, and he resigned from the army at age 23.

Then he fell in love. At one of the leading salons of Paris, where the young Marquis was constantly in demand, he met a dainty American, Medora von Hoffman, daughter of a German baron who had become a wealthy New York banker. Medora was easy on the eyes—five feet tall, delicate, with pale skin and glossy deep-red hair. But of the two, Morès was more striking. He was six feet tall and weighed a sinewy 170 pounds, with curly black hair and brilliant eyes under imperious, slightly drooping eyelids; he wore a mustache that he waxed to points as sharp as the tip of a dart. The Marquis proposed to Medora in the rose garden of the Von Hoffman villa in Cannes, and on February 15, 1882, with the blue waters of the Mediterranean sparkling below them, they were married by the Bishop of Fréjus in the stained-glass chapel of La Verrière.

The new Marquise and her husband spent the next several months on a honeymoon. In August they sailed for the United States and, with their five personal servants, took up residence at the Von Hoffman home on Staten Island. The Marquis began commuting to Wall Street to learn the business at his father-in-law's bank. Morès, with his keen mind and capacity for work, steeped himself in finance, only to learn that banking and trading, especially in a slow market, were just too dull for his blood.

Day after day, as he tediously pored over investment reports, the Marquis came to think that there must be a more fulfilling way for a nobleman to make his mark in American commerce. The only materials he could find that held his interest were some glowing reports on investment possibilities in the cattle business out West. Ranching, Morès came to realize, was assuming the proportions of an international craze.

"The West! The mighty West!" gushed author James S. Brisbin in a book that was popular at the time, *The Beef Bonanza; or, How to Get Rich on the Plains.* "That land where the buffalo still roams and the wild savage dwells; where the broad rivers flow and the boundless prairie stretches away for thousands of miles; where the poor, professional young man, flying from the overcrowded East and the tyranny of a moneyed aristocracy, finds honor and wealth!" Invariably, Brisbin and other enthusiasts overlooked the debits of ranching, such as climatic risks, while grossly exaggerating the credits, such as the nutritive properties of the brown bunch grass on Dakota prairies.

Morès knew something of this land. His cousin, known only as Count Fitz-James, had spent the fall of 1882 hunting in the Badlands of Dakota and had returned to tell the Marquis of the region's great potential. Morès began to dig deeper into the subject. The beef business was booming, and foreigners were jumping on the wagon. Investors in England and Scotland alone had channeled some $30 million into Western cattle. Foreign interests controlled nearly 20 million acres of range land in the Great Plains.

The Marquis de Morès began to draft a grandiose plan. From newspaper accounts he learned that ranchers were shipping their cattle in bulk at great expense to Chicago, where middlemen butchers like Philip D. Armour and Gustavus Swift were making fortunes with their slaughterhouses. The dressed beef was then packed off in refrigerator cars bound for the East — or all the way back to the growing markets in the West.

Surely, Morès reasoned, a cattleman's profit could be vastly expanded by eliminating the middlemen. Why not construct a slaughtering and meat-dressing plant right on the range?

Researching this notion, the Frenchman concluded that the economic virtues of slaughtering on the spot made shipping cattle on the hoof look like an inefficient practice at best. As only 40 per cent of a cow was edible, the cattleman who shipped his stock live was spending 60 per cent more for transportation than was necessary. The Marquis took his case to his millionaire father-in-law. Von Hoffman was impressed and offered financial support. Thus bolstered, Morès bade goodbye to his wife; he and his valet packed suitable expedition gear, including a small arsenal and some wines that traveled well, and boarded a train for the Badlands. He was not the only man to see the possibilities of a dressed-meat plant in the West (at that moment, three were being constructed in Texas and ground was being broken for another near Cheyenne, Wyoming), but no cattleman anywhere would ever match Morès for gusto.

His initial look at the Badlands, on that first day out astride a rented horse, convinced the Marquis he had found the proper place. As he and his valet Van Driesche roamed the Little Missouri Valley, they saw that the region's topography and vegetation were perfect for livestock. On the open prairies bunch grass, or buffalo grass as it was called locally, grew in abundance and would provide ample grazing. Cattle could find shelter from storms in the deep draws and coulees, as well as in the thickets of chokecherry bushes, ash, plum, box elder and cottonwood trees.

At midday Morès halted his ride at a small stream and Van Driesche cooled a bottle of white wine in the water. Then the valet fetched from his saddlebags *pâté de foie gras,* sardines, potted meat, cheese and bread. Using a flat rock for a table, the two men ate all they had and stretched out in the sun. The Marquis, fully aware that where he lay was close to a major new railroad line at the easternmost edge of America's cattle-ranching range, decided that he had discovered a beautiful and practical place for doing business.

He quickly learned that these assets, along with game so plentiful it could be shot at from the railroad cars, had attracted others to the region before him.

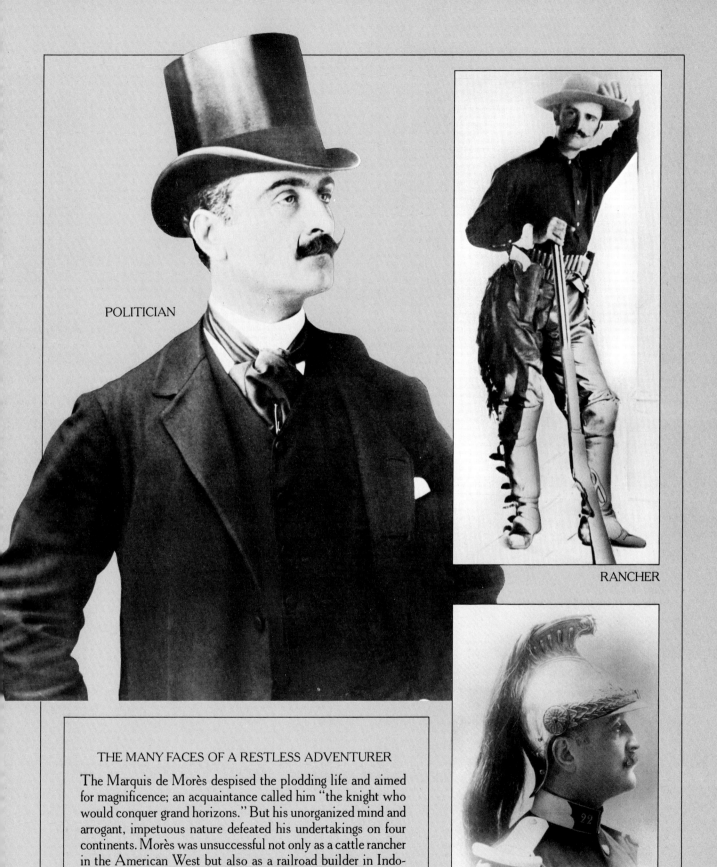

POLITICIAN

RANCHER

DRAGOON

THE MANY FACES OF A RESTLESS ADVENTURER

The Marquis de Morès despised the plodding life and aimed for magnificence; an acquaintance called him "the knight who would conquer grand horizons." But his unorganized mind and arrogant, impetuous nature defeated his undertakings on four continents. Morès was unsuccessful not only as a cattle rancher in the American West but also as a railroad builder in Indochina, as a politician endeavoring to topple the French Republic and as a soldier attempting to oust the British from Egypt.

Medora von Hoffman was the daughter of a German baron, married a French marquis and reigned like a princess over the town named for her. She painted, played Beethoven and was a crack rifle shot.

Among the various ranchers, professional hunters and frontier drifters, several individuals stood out. Two brothers from Pittsburgh, Howard and Alden Eaton, had arrived in 1879 and set up a cattle operation; their ranch was the first in the West to take in paying dudes. Henry Boice had come from New Mexico to start a successful cattle company, known by its brand as the 777; a Scotsman, Gregor Lang, had arrived to manage the cattle interests of an Englishman named Sir John Pender. Still, the Marquis found there was choice land left, and after three days of riding, covering about 50 miles a day, he started to make arrangements for the purchase of property.

With $15,000 worth of government scrip he had purchased from his father-in-law, Morès bought 220 acres that gave him access to the river and to the railroad. This parcel included land just to the south of Little Missouri and the land directly across the river to the east on which his tent was pitched. In addition, he paid the Northern Pacific Railroad $23,314 for nearly 9,000 acres a few miles out of town, which he planned to use as his own private range. Morès then quickly spent about $36,000 for cattle, stocking his range with more than 10,000 head. He also began contracting with local ranchers to raise sheep for him on a commission basis. For this operation he anticipated buying about 9,600 head. At the same time Morès purchased about 200 brood mares, as well as a few fine stallions.

To celebrate this auspicious entrance into the West, the Marquis, with his valet standing at attention beside him, cracked a bottle of wine on an iron tent peg. Then, with the lights from Little Misery twinkling across the river before them, the two men toasted the ground on which they stood, and Morès christened the site after his wife, Medora. To her, back in New York, the Marquis wrote: "I like this country for there is room to move about without stepping on the feet of others."

Before long the slumbering Badlands awoke to a tidal wave of activity inspired by Morès. Carloads of building materials arrived on the Northern Pacific, and with them came carpenters, masons and special construction crews. Along a spur track built from the main line there began to rise what would later be a quarter-million-dollar slaughterhouse crammed with the latest equipment, flanked by corrals for cattle and topped by a towering smokestack of yellowish brick. Housing was started for the plant's employees, along with a general store, a company office, a hotel and recreation hall containing bowling alleys and billiard rooms. Saloonkeepers, including more than one entrepreneur from Little Misery, moved across the river to slake the workers' thirst. Inevitably, competition between the old settlement and the growing new one reached fever pitch. "The air fairly seethed with rivalry and factional feeling," Gregor Lang's son, Lincoln, later recalled. "Like a pair of bulldogs on a leash, aching to be at each other's throats, the two communities glowered at each other from opposite sides of the river." With the money Morès was pouring into it, Medora clearly seemed the better bet.

Living under canvas hardly suited the Marquis' sensibilities, so he soon arranged to rent a luxurious private railroad car, the Montana, for $15 a day. From this headquarters he sallied forth to supervise and urge on his workers, but in slower moments callers were welcome to stop by the car for a little "something for the snake bite," such as a glass of excellent brandy. Morès also used his spare time to oversee the building of more permanent lodging: a king-sized, two-story ranch house of 26 rooms that was being rushed to completion so the Marquise and their infant daughter could be properly housed. The site for the Château de Morès was a high bluff across the river to the west, commanding a superb view of the town and the countryside the Marquis was bringing under his control. The first work done on the house, of course, was the excavation for the wine cellar.

With his father-in-law's generous backing, plus a promise of support—but no interference—from an official of the Northern Pacific Railroad, Morès made elaborate plans to keep his burgeoning empire under his thumb. He formed the Northern Pacific Refrigerator Car Company, capitalized at $200,000; of the 2,000 shares, issued with a par value of $100 each, the Marquis and Von Hoffman retained more than enough for control. Morès listed the firm's main objective as the slaughter and sale of cattle, sheep and hogs; as a sideline, the company would transport produce on a contract basis. Then, with royal self-confidence,

fort," as its waggish owner put it, a barbershop and a bathhouse, a brickmaking plant, a book and confectionery shop, a doctor and a drugstore, a blacksmith shop, a billiard parlor, a Chinese laundry and a place called J. S. Warn's Oyster Grotto that claimed to offer the best in Western cuisine. Medora also had gained a newspaper, the *Bad Lands Cow Boy*.

High on a bluff above the thriving village lived the Morès family in splendor so lordly it suggested frontier feudalism. Few freight trains pulled into Medora without at least one shipment bound for the château: art supplies from Knoedler's Galleries; silver pieces from Tiffany; furniture from Lord & Taylor; capers, plovers' eggs, queen olives, canned truffles, mushrooms and meringues from Park & Tilford; and sherries, burgundies, champagnes and the Marquis' favorite wine, Château Lagrange, from the Saint-Julien district of Bordeaux. Morès seldom condescended to dine with his neighbors near Medora, more than half of whom were his employees, because their conversation was not likely to stimulate him. But he made an exception in the case of Theodore Roosevelt. Roosevelt was a frequent visitor to the château when he was in the Badlands, and the Marquis reciprocated when he was in New York.

Each seems to have enjoyed the other's company, until the summer of 1885, when they had their first disagreement. The Marquis had contracted to buy a herd of Roosevelt's cattle at the Chicago price minus 70 cents per head. Roosevelt delivered the beef to the Marquis' yards, received a check and discovered that the figure was half a cent less per pound than he had been promised. The Marquis explained that the prices had dropped in the Chicago market, thus the reduction in the payment. Roosevelt insisted that he was due the higher price that was agreed on earlier. Here, said Medora newspaper editor Arthur Packard, who was present as the argument heated up, "the situation got a little bit tense." Finally, Roosevelt cut off the quarrel by ordering his cattle removed from the stockyard. Henceforth, he said, he would sell in Chicago. For the next few months, the two proud men went their separate ways, each saying little, if anything, about the episode.

Meanwhile, persistent friends of the young William Riley Luffsey, who had been killed in the Me-

dora gunfight two summers earlier, finally succeeded in getting the Marquis indicted in Mandan for first-degree murder. The two previous court actions against Morès had been only hearings; this time there would be a trial. A change of venue placed the proceedings in Bismarck, 10 miles from Mandan. The Marquis was placed in the county jail, convinced that he had been railroaded and, moreover, that some of Roosevelt's men, including Joe Ferris, had contributed to the railroading. After four days of simmering in a cell, Morès wrote:

My dear Roosevelt:

My principle is to take the bull by the horns. Joe Ferris is very active against me and has been instrumental in getting me indicted by furnishing money to witnesses and hunting them up. The papers also publish very stupid accounts of our quarrelling—I sent you the paper in New York. Is this done by your orders? I thought you were my friend. If you are my enemy I want to know it. I am always on hand as you know, and between gentlemen it is easy to settle matters of that sort directly.

Yours very truly,
Morès

The letter at first confused Roosevelt. Was Morès implying that they settle the matter by a duel? He read it aloud to Bill Sewall. If the Marquis was challenging him, Sewall recalled Roosevelt as saying, then "he should accept the challenge, for he would not be bullied. He said that his friends would all be opposed to his fighting a duel, and that he was opposed to dueling himself. But if he was challenged, he should accept. That would give him the choice of weapons. He would choose Winchester rifles, and have the distance arranged at twelve paces. He did not consider himself a very good shot and wanted to be near enough so that he could hit. They would shoot and advance until one or the other was satisfied."

Roosevelt's reply, written the following day, was admirably punctilious:

Dear de Morès:

Most emphatically I am not your enemy; if I were you would know it, for I would be an open one, and would not have asked you to my house nor gone to yours. As your final words, howev-

174

Theodore Roosevelt's eight-room Elkhorn ranch house on the Little Missouri River near Medora was spacious enough to accommodate the families of his two stewards from Maine. Completed in the spring of 1885, the house was constructed of cottonwood timbers, for which Roosevelt himself chopped down 17 trees in three days.

er, seem to imply a threat it is due to myself to say that the statement is not made through any fear of possible consequences to me; I too, as you know, am always on hand, and ever ready to hold myself accountable in any way for anything I have said or done.

Upon receiving this, the Marquis drafted a conciliatory note. He amended his first letter to say that there was always a way for gentlemen to settle their differences—"without trouble."

Satisfied, Roosevelt visited Morès in his cell to assure him that their relationship was mutually respectful. To Roosevelt, the Marquis appeared not the least bit apprehensive about the outcome of his trial; nor, as it turned out, should he have been. The proceedings lasted a week; the jury took one ballot and returned a verdict of not guilty. Not long after Morès was released, Bill Sewall reported, "he invited Theodore to his house to dinner. Theodore went and once more everything passed off pleasantly."

Though the Marquis did not say so publicly, the two and a half years he had spent in the Badlands had taken a heavy toll. For Roosevelt the experience had been marvelous. For Morès, who had suffered a long, bitter legal battle and the enmity of many neighbors, it had been an ordeal, and by the next year it could be called a disaster. The day was near when both men would end the Western chapter of their lives.

Roosevelt, in his heart, would always remain a rancher, hunter, cowboy and defender of the right, but gradually other matters began to claim his time. Principal among them was Edith Carow, whom he married late in 1886 and installed in his new house in Oyster Bay, New York. That same winter, blizzards in the Badlands virtually wiped out Roosevelt's stock, as well as most of his neighbors'. During a visit to determine his losses when the weather warmed in April, Roosevelt wrote his sister Corinne: "I am bluer than indigo about the cattle. It is even worse than I feared; I wish I was sure I would lose no more than half the money I invested out here. I am planning how to get out of it." From then on, politics consumed the majority of Roosevelt's interests and energy.

Morès' life took quite a different turn. He had made magnificent plans, and for a while they actually

seemed to work. Remarkably, his slaughterhouse was operating just five months after the first brick had been laid, and during the first season the Marquis' butchers were dressing up 80 beef a day. The following year only marginal slaughtering was done because the cattle never quite reached prime condition. Morès hung his hopes on 1885 and projected slaughtering 20,000 head with daily sales of $6,000. By the beginning of the season he had built, at a cost of $150,000, cold storage and icing stations at a dozen points along the railroad from Chicago to Helena, Montana. Unfortunately, most of his stock did not fatten enough to be killed, largely because the grass that year was not as plentiful as it had been in summers past when there had been more rain. After temporarily closing the plant once while waiting for the cattle to fatten, Morès ended the slaughtering season two months early, and though he did not make the figures public, fell disturbingly short of his announced goal. Still the Frenchman refused to yield.

"There was something gorgeous in the Marquis' inability to know when he was beaten," as the rancher Howard Eaton remembered. "His power of self-hypnotism was amazing."

In 1886, in his continuing attempt to bypass middlemen and to lower prices, Morès began to establish his own retail outlets to deliver his meat "from the ranch to the table," as he advertised. In New York he was instrumental in organizing the National Consumers Meat Company, capitalized at $10 million in shares of $10 each. After announcing that "the city slaughterers cannot compete with us," the Marquis opened six butcher shops and offered at reduced prices beef shipped directly from Medora. But the capital Morès expected to raise from New York investors never materialized; all the shops were closed not long after their grand openings.

The Marquis' restless mind produced an array of other schemes. Noting that West Coast salmon was becoming a great delicacy, he had arranged in 1884 to buy the catch of commercial fisheries in Oregon, pack it in his refrigerator cars and have it on the best New York dinner tables, fresh, in a matter of days. Before he was through, he would be able to say he had also tried sheep raising, had offered his grain lands to farmers on attractive terms and had even imported expert truck gardeners from New Jersey to raise cabbages and other vegetables under glass before transplanting and forcing them to early maturity with fertilizer made from the offal of his slaughterhouse. In the midst of all this, he started his own stagecoach line from Medora to Deadwood, 215 miles to the south.

Every one of these ideas failed and the dream came apart. Morès, for all of his acumen, absorbed nothing of the economics of any of his enterprises and that, as much as anything, brought down his empire. Most of his sheep died; someone had sold him a breed incapable of surviving a Dakota winter. His stage line did well at first, then faded after Morès failed to get a U.S. mail contract to undergird the operation. To top it off, the cattle market started to go bad, and established packers, wholesalers, retailers and the railroad combined to push Morès' shaky operation toward a strangling death.

Then came the blizzards of 1886-1887—the long-remembered "Die-Up" that ruined Roosevelt's investment and destroyed cattle herds all around the overstocked, overgrazed Northern Plains. The Marquis lost no cattle to the weather because he had stopped raising his own beef in 1885, preferring to buy stock from other ranchers. But the season after the blizzards there was little stock to buy.

Morès wanted to go on fighting, but his banker father-in-law called a halt. In four years the two men had lost between one and two million dollars. The packing plant never opened for the 1887 season. The town of Medora began to shrivel; wooden houses that could be moved were uprooted and placed on flatcars to ship to more promising settlements. A number of townspeople moved away. Morès moved too, taking his family to Paris for the winter. The house in Medora was left fully stocked and furnished for his return the next year. But the Marquis never came back.

In Paris, undismayed by the failure of his American adventure, he cast about for new opportunities. "Every lane has its turning," he is reported to have said. "A man without ambition is good for nothing. There must be an aim in life, always higher. I am 28 years old. I am strong as a horse. I want to play a real part. I am ready to start again."

At the end of 1887 the Marquis and the Marquise went tiger hunting in Nepal, Medora enthusiastically bagging her share while perched on the back of an elephant. On the voyage home from India, Morès ran into old classmates from Saint-Cyr and Saumur who had been fighting in the French protectorate of Tonkin and whose tales tempted him with the region's commercial possibilities. Inspired, Morès went off to Indochina to construct a railroad. Within a year he was back in France, having failed at the complex game of international intrigue. In Paris he launched a movement based on a combination of socialism and anti-Semitism with the hope of fomenting a nationalist uprising. To attract attention to his cause, the Marquis and his supporters went around attired in cowboy shirts and ten-gallon hats.

In the spring of 1896 the "cowboy from France" went on one last adventure. This time it was to the wild frontier of North Africa, where he aimed to persuade Islamic tribes to join the French in driving the British out of Egypt; in the process he hoped to repair his own tattered political and financial position. Morès' caravan—camels, horses, wagons, interpreter, drivers, guides—set out from the shores of the Mediterranean to explore a military route 3,000 miles across the Sahara to the Upper Nile, which he hoped could be used eventually as an avenue of attack against the British. But on the morning of June 9, after traveling 200 miles, Morès' party was attacked by bands of Tuareg and Chambaa tribesmen on a desolate plain called El Ouatia.

In the first assault, the Marquis was struck with a saber on the wrist. Gushing blood, he drew his Colt revolver, killed one assailant and drove off the rest. Then Morès took cover and sniped away at the encircling enemy in a final, Western-style shoot-out that lasted two hours. He was on his knees, still reloading and firing, when a Chambaa came up behind him and stabbed him between his shoulder blades. The Marquis de Morès went down, five days short of his 38th birthday and a long, long way from his beloved Medora and the Badlands empire of his dreams.

As for Roosevelt, he returned to the Dakota Badlands during one of his campaign swings in 1900. "I had studied a lot about men and things before I saw you fellows," he stated, looking out on a tableau of leathery faces. "But it was only when I came here that I began to know anything, or measure men rightly."

Western hospitality for fun and profit

Ranchers in the West could be counted on to offer a hot meal and a bunk to anyone caught on the trail at dusk. Even so, the Eaton brothers, Howard, Willis and Alden, were more hospitable than most. To their Custer Trail Ranch, set up in Dakota Territory in 1879, they welcomed not only neighbors but also a stream of visitors recruited on frequent trips back East.

No guest paid for his keep until 1882, when one dude, desiring to postpone his departure, arranged to stay on for the price of his board and the use of a horse. Soon paying guests produced more profit than stock raising, and the dude ranch was born.

The Eatons kept a hand in raising stock, however. After moving the ranch in 1904 to Wolf, Wyoming, they ran a "working ranch." It served well as an authentic background for activities and entertainments designed for a tenderfoot's taste and capability.

Wranglers corral horses in a 1909 photograph of the Eaton ranch in Wyoming. Low buildings between the barns are cottages for dudes.

Part of the Eaton clan gathers together in front of the Custer Trail ranch house in 1890. Soon afterward, they sold out and began a search for a more picturesque—and lucrative—location.

Showing off for guests, Alden Eaton's son, Bill, holds on tight as a dude prepares to remove a blindfold from a bucking mule on the Eatons' Wyoming ranch in 1905. The mule was virtually unridable and once the calming blindfold came off, the plucky showman usually hit the dirt.

A column of Eaton riders, out for a few weeks of camping, follows a stream in Yellowstone National Park, 200 miles from the ranch. On these leisurely outings, as many as 50 vacationers rode to the park on a train that carried horses, saddles, tents and a crew of wranglers to do the work.

Amid bedding spread out to air, a clutch of lady dudes—
and one stolid husband—crochet and chat after a campfire
breakfast as they await their horses for the day's excursion.
As soon as the guests departed, camp tenders struck the
two-person tents, loaded beds and baggage into wagons
and hurried ahead of their charges to set up the next camp.

185

Eaton dudes enjoy a break from the saddle at Iceberg Lake in Glacier National Park, snowbound the year round except July and August. Scenery like this, fresh mountain air and good Western company induced some guests to tarry at the Eaton ranch for months. The Eatons' spread was a model for dozens of dude ranches throughout the West.

187

6 | "Behold our ditches!"

From its Spanish beginnings California was a rancher's dream, a "perfect paradise" for grazing livestock and for growing an astonishing variety of crops. "In the hands of an enterprising people," wrote Richard Henry Dana in 1840, "what a country this might be!" Once the gold rush brought enterprising people in abundance, only one elusive commodity was needed to fulfill the California dream: water.

Much of the new state was subject to severe droughts, often followed by crippling floods, which defeated more than one rancher. If California was to become more than just a patchwork of ranches clustered on the banks of rivers, a way would have to be found to make water more widely available.

The concept of irrigation had been brought to California by Spanish padres as early as 1769. The technique was little used until the influx of gold rushers created an urgent need for more food and more arable land. Ranchers began diverting water from rivers, drilling artesian and pump wells and digging reservoirs. They were so proud of the result that in 1859 *Hutchings' California Magazine* proclaimed: "Behold our ditches!"

Soon one out of four California ranches was irrigated. Kern County, sweltering at the southern end of San Joaquin Valley, experienced an irrigation boom spectacular even by California standards. The ranchers dug 300 miles of canals from the Kern River and sank 40 artesian wells whose free-flowing fountains of clear, pure water turned half a million acres of dry dirt into some of the richest land anywhere.

A Kern County family in the 1880s uses an artesian well to irrigate the thirsty land. The well tapped a 50-mile-long underground river flowing from the Sierras.

Well-bred cattle amble from a well to a pasture on the Jackson Ranch located in Kern County. Canal-irrigated and served by artesian wells, the ranch grew alfalfa for its herds and produced giant harvests of corn, oats and barley.

The rich and varied yield of the abundantly watered Lakeside Ranch near Bakersfield—the ranch grew everything from cattle to 27-pound sweet potatoes—is reflected in this early-morning view of its yard. The artesian well at right center, shielded by a roof, was one of five on the ranch; it produced 30,000 gallons of "splendid" water each day.

Members of the Crocker family of Kern County enjoy the shade of poplars and elms planted in a careful row hard by their ranch house in the 1880s. Water from wells provided midsummer relief when temperatures reached 110°F.

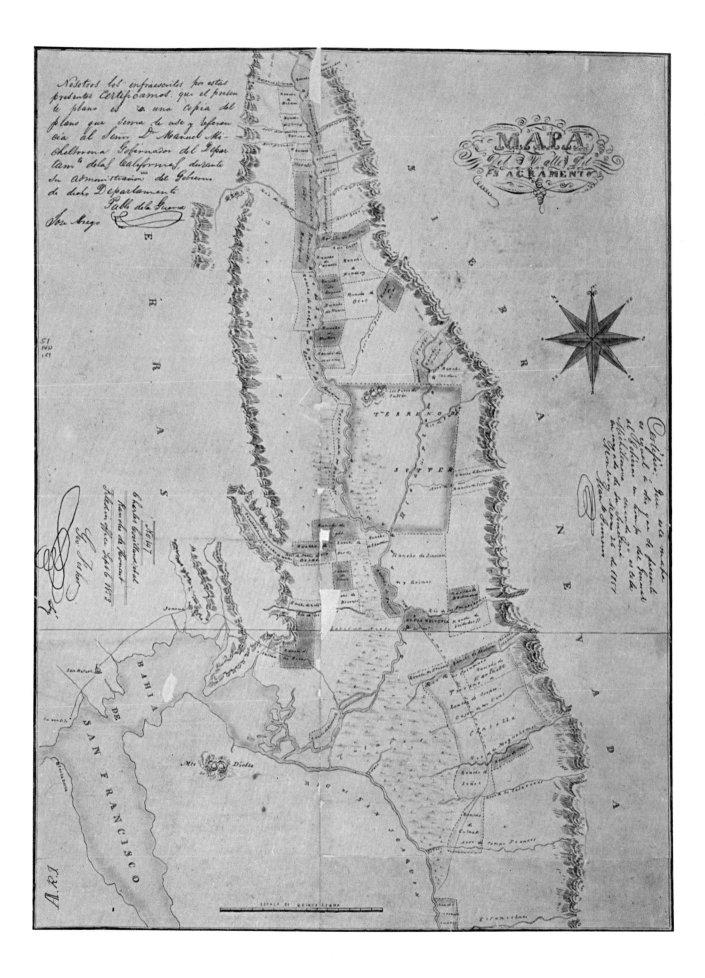

Land of abundance for the ultimate ranchers

Decades before cattle ranching spread north from Texas across the Great Plains, ranching of a different sort was flourishing lazily in the Mexican province of California. Besides livestock, the early California ranchers raised crops of all kinds, and in their fertile lands and usually benign climate, apples grew to the size of pumpkins.

As early as the 1820s and 1830s, Americans were beginning to learn of the exotic foreign province far across the empty plains and rugged mountains. A handful of returning traders and trappers sang California's praises in frontier settlements along the Mississippi and Missouri rivers, awakening dreams of an earthly paradise among hard-put homesteaders who cared nothing about ranching as such. The frontiersmen yearned to raise crops all year round on a piece of that incredibly rich California land, and they longed to escape the wintertime fevers and agues that tormented them in Iowa and Missouri and Illinois.

A trader named Antoine Robidoux, just back from the West Coast Eden in 1840, practically guaranteed a gathering of awed Missourians that California's generous government would give them more land than they could possibly till. According to John Bidwell, a 21-year-old schoolmaster in the group, Robidoux also vouched for the perfection of California's weather, declaring: "There was but one man that ever had a chill there, and it was a matter of so much wonderment to the people of Monterey that they went eighteen miles into the country to see him shake."

Young Bidwell, a would-be farmer with a brilliant future in ranching, succumbed to California's allures in the spring of 1841 and joined the first party of migrant settlers to make the 2,000-mile overland journey. After groping their way westward for six arduous months, Bidwell and 31 comrades arrived in California—though they did not realize it until they had almost reached the coast and came, in early November, upon the isolated ranch of an American settler in the northwestern corner of the San Joaquin Valley.

California, at first blush, appeared to be something less than heaven on earth. "It had been one of the driest years ever known in California," Bidwell reported in his memoirs many years later. "The country was brown and parched. Cattle were almost starving for grass." Shortly after their arrival, the winter rains began, and "streams were out of their banks; gulches were swimming; plains were inundated." In less than one month, Bidwell had seen the extremes of "perfect" California weather—extremes that repeatedly whipsawed the ranchers and ruined years of hard labor. Yet whenever the land got just enough water, it was as fertile as any in the world.

Bidwell received his introduction to ranching, California style, in the Sacramento Valley on a large land grant *(opposite)* owned by John Augustus Sutter, a Swiss immigrant who, seven years later, was to be credited with starting the California gold rush. The hearty rancher, "one of the most liberal and hospitable of men," gave Bidwell a warm welcome—and a much-needed job as an assistant. As the seasons changed in their subtle California way, Bidwell was continually surprised by the grand scale and sheer variety of Sutter's enterprises. One startling scene of a wheat harvest—so primitive and yet so ambitious—stuck in Bidwell's memory as the epitome of Sutter's approach to ranching.

"Imagine," Bidwell urged the readers of his memoirs, "three or four hundred wild Indians in a grain-

This 1844 map of Sacramento Valley was drawn by John Bidwell to show the lands of his employer, John Sutter. Bidwell himself soon became a major rancher.

field, armed, some with sickles, some with butcher knives, some with pieces of hoop iron roughly fashioned into shapes like sickles, but many having only their hands with which to gather up the dry and brittle grain." To Bidwell, "the wildest part was the threshing." After the wheat had been piled high in a round corral, "three or four hundred wild horses were turned in to thresh it, the Indians whooping to make them run faster." From time to time, Indians dashed in front of the mustangs to make them change direction: "The movement was reversed, with the effect of plowing up the trampled straw. In this manner I have seen 2,000 bushels of wheat threshed in a single hour."

Sutter's veritable army of ranch hands—mostly Indians with some Mexicans and a few foreigners—included *vaqueros* to manage 12,000 cattle and 2,000 horses, herders to tend and shear 10,000 sheep, gardeners to cultivate the fields of vegetables, orchardmen to plant and care for assorted fruit trees and tanners who processed hides. There also were weavers to make woolen blankets, trappers and hunters to bring in pelts from the game-rich wilderness, woodsmen to fell trees and saw lumber, and later, millwrights and a distiller.

As Bidwell came to realize, nothing quite like these great California ranches existed anywhere else. In the East, Northern farms and even Southern plantations were rarely larger than 3,000 acres—less than one tenth the size of Sutter's domain; their owners concentrated heavily on cash crops, and although thousands of them did raise small numbers of cattle and sheep for meat, they did so as a sideline. Big-time ranching in the West—in Texas and on the Northern Plains—was stock raising pure and simple; no crops were grown on a commercial basis, though many cattle barons did plant enough corn to fatten their steers for market. By contrast, ranching in California benefited hugely from the fact that its first settlers had raised both livestock and a wonderful variety of crops.

When ranchers in the mid-19th Century were faced with swiftly changing conditions, the more innovative drew upon this heritage and simply shifted the emphasis of their operations. This flexibility proved crucial, for they had to contend with faster and more radical change than did the settlers anywhere else in the West. California was, as a San Francisco chron-

icler wrote in 1855, "a hot-bed that brought humanity to a rapid, monstrous maturity, like the mammoth vegetables for which it is so celebrated."

The discovery of gold in John Sutter's millrace triggered an unprecedented mass migration and created a desperate shortage of food as the non-Indian population of California expanded from approximately 14,000 in 1848 to a quarter of a million in 1852. But the ranchers, who found that they could sell almost anything to the legion of hungry gold prospectors, met the challenge and then some. For a time any kind of meat was difficult to come by in the gold fields. Then the ranchers rebuilt their depleted cattle herds—mostly with Texas longhorns—and they rebuilt them so rapidly that shortly they were overproducing for even their swollen market. In little more than a decade they had three million head of cattle, and some of the surplus was exported to stock new ranches in Oregon and the Northern Plains.

Cattle raising was itself overshadowed in a few years by wheat growing, a much more profitable operation. And the reign of wheat was short-lived, too; the wheat fields soon gave way to seas of vegetables and enormous vistas of vineyards and orchards. Over the years, the progressive ranchers steadily brought more and more land under cultivation; they combated drought with an expanding network of irrigation canals and upgraded their stock with scientific breeding—always increasing the productivity of their acreage. They were the first Western experts in large-scale land management, and by the end of the 19th Century, they had developed their prodigal fields into giant food factories and produced agricultural wealth that was the wonder of the world.

As late as 1880, the California ranchers' shift of emphasis from cattle raising to intensive farming seemed to have no relevance for the Great Plains. Ranchers from Texas to the Canadian border had vastly more land for expansion than the Californians, and their territories and states were filling with settlers at a slower rate. In fact, however, the transformation of California ranching was a harbinger of things to come in the Great Plains as well. Even in areas less fertile than California's valleys, farmers could produce more food per acre than stockmen. To make farming prospects even more tempting, distant markets for

food were increasing rapidly in size and accessibility.

California-style ranching would make deep inroads into the domains of Texas-style cattle ranching. Indeed, the future arrived sooner rather than later. More than a few veteran Plains cattlemen—pioneers who had opened new lands for settlement, who had fought Indians, barbed wire and farmers—saw their ranch lands bear many of the crops that astonished John Bidwell on Sutter's ranch back in 1842.

California's pattern of diversified ranching was set by its first colonists, Catholic missionaries from Spanish Mexico. Starting in 1769, small groups of Franciscan priests founded a chain of 21 missions that stretched 650 miles up the coast from San Diego to San Francisco Bay. The padres came with Mexican cattle, horses, sheep, pigs, seeds and cuttings from fruit trees and vines, and they built up great ranching fiefdoms.

Much of their mission land was given over to livestock, but their Indian converts also grew wheat, barley, maize, squashes, rice, beans, lentils and peas, and brought in bountiful harvests of grapes, apples, pears, peaches, figs, olives, melons and citrus fruits.

Since the land seemed limitless and was therefore without market value, the Franciscans counted their wealth in cattle. Their herds, left to graze and breed at random, paid them compound interest. By the 1820s even the small Mission Nuestra Senora de la Soledad in the Salinas Valley had 15,000 head of livestock. An American scout, reconnoitering California in 1829, reported that the Mission San Gabriel Arcángel, east of the tiny settlement of Los Angeles, had 70,000 cattle, 4,200 horses and 400 mules.

Like the early Spanish ranchers in Texas, the padres had almost no local market for their beef and no means of preserving the meat for long-distance shipment; but they, too, sent Mexico a modest volume of hides from their lean longhorns. Their business broadened after 1821, when Mexico won its independence from Spain. The new government relaxed the old Spanish restriction against dealing with foreigners and opened California ports to the ships of several nations. Soon the California trade was dominated by American vessels from aggressive mercantile houses in Boston. Yankee ships brought manufactured goods to the coastal ranches and the few villages that had grown up around the missions. They sailed home around Cape Horn with California hides for making leather goods and rendered fat for making soap and tallow candles.

In 1833 an anticlerical Mexican government secularized the rich California missions, ordering that half of each mission's land and cattle be made available for private claim, with the rest—supposedly—to be turned over to the Franciscans' Indian wards. Predictably, most of the mission lands, plus immense tracts of virgin wilderness, passed into the hands of political and military officials, and their relatives and friends. The Pico family, which boasted a California governor among its members, claimed more than 700,000 acres. The 14 claims filed by the de la Guerra family totaled 488,329 acres, the Castros got 280,000 acres and the Yorbas 218,000 acres. General Mariano Vallejo obtained a major part of the Sonoma Valley and stocked his estates with 50,000 cattle, 24,000 sheep and 8,000 horses. The aristocrats built substantial houses on their land and led leisurely lives of rustic elegance.

These great estates—and the wealthy rancheros' unwed daughters—put ambitious notions into the

A PICTORIAL PETITION FOR LAND
The Rancho San Miguelito de la Trinidad, located in the Santa Lucia Range near Monterey, was crudely but clearly defined in this 1841 map, which Lieutenant José Rafael Gonzalez submitted to the governor of Mexican California as part of his petition for the property. The ranch's identifying features, coded by number, include the Nacimiento River (4), a creek (20), a spring (5), and several roads or trails. Besides producing such a plan, the applicant for a land grant had only to prove that no one else owned the property and, after his petition was approved, to build a house on the land and start stock raising within a year. Gonzalez, who had political pull as the chief customs official at Monterey, was granted his ranch in 1842.

Abel Stearns, a tough, wealthy veteran
who ranched near Los Angeles, had a battle scar at the corner of his mouth. He got
it—and nearly lost his life—in a bloody
knife fight with a sailor in the 1830s.

heads of foreign traders, mariners and others who
reached California. Since acreage could be had almost
for the asking by foreigners who became Mexican
citizens, dozens of fortune hunters took up residence
in some convenient port of call, joined the Catholic
Church, pledged allegiance to Mexico, acquired land
grants and wooed the maiden heiresses of their lordly
neighbors. Though their attentions were often unwelcome, some triumphed. In Santa Barbara, Bostonian
Alfred Robinson (Don José María Alfredo) married
the daughter of Captain José Antonio de la Guerra. In
Los Angeles, Benjamin Wilson (Don Benito) won
the hand of Ramona Yorba, and John Temple (Don
Juan) espoused Doña Rafaela Cota.

At least one Yankee in the market for marriage,
Abel Stearns, was no fortune hunter; he was looking
for a California bride to cap his already extravagantly
successful career. A native of Lunenburg, Massachusetts, Stearns had gone to sea at the age of 12 and
worked his way up to the post of supercargo—the
owner's representative—on ships trading with China
and South America. In 1827 he gave up the sea to
begin a new career in Mexico, became a naturalized
citizen and eventually settled in Los Angeles. There
Stearns set himself up as a merchant, buying furs from
American trappers working the Rockies and trading
Yankee dry goods and liquors for hides and tallow
from the rancheros. Don Abel was the wealthiest
merchant in southern California when he selected the
dark-eyed beauty who was to be his wife. She was
Arcadia Bandini, and her rancher father was honored
to accept him as a son-in-law—no matter that Stearns
was in his forties and Arcadia was just 14.

Soon after his marriage (which proved to be a
happy one despite the age difference) Don Abel
bought the 26,000-acre Rancho Los Alamitos, reportedly for $6,000, and began building an enormous
empire. He put into land and cattle his profits from his
trading business and from high-interest loans to other
rancheros, including one to his father-in-law, who fell
into debt to a gambler. Including the holdings he had
acquired as his bride's dowry, Stearns at the peak of
his career in the early 1860s owned a dozen ranches
totaling more than 200,000 acres.

John Sutter, on whose ranch John Bidwell got his
start, was another early immigrant who shared

Stearns's ambition, though eventually not his success.
Sutter, a glib merchant born in Germany of Swiss
parents, had fled to the New World as a young man
to escape his creditors. He arrived in California in
1839 with money to invest after sundry ventures and
travels in New Mexico, the Rockies, Hawaii and
Alaska. The Mexican governor of California gave
him permission to reconnoiter land on which to set up
a colony. Sutter's selection of a site, which he made
on a boat trip up the Sacramento River, was daring in
the extreme. On a claim of some 50,000 acres, he
planted the first settlement in the California heartland,
a great trough between the coastal mountains and the
Sierra Nevada through which the Sacramento and
San Joaquin rivers flowed. Known later as Central
Valley, it eventually proved to comprise 16 million
acres of the richest land on earth.

By 1841 Sutter was over his head in ambitious
undertakings. His colony, devoted to farming, was
still being built on one part of his grant, near the
confluence of the Sacramento and American rivers; he

named this section New Helvetia, but it was more widely known as Sutter's Fort. On the larger part of his domain, along the Feather River near the mouth of Bear Creek, he began a farming and livestock ranch called Hock Farm. He had contracted to buy—for $2,000 down and $30,000 on credit—a woebegone Russian colony called Fort Ross, north of San Francisco. The Russians had founded the colony in 1812 to raise food for their province of Alaska. Throughout their occupation the California government had been too weak to oust them, and finally the Russians' own weakness had prompted them to abandon the losing venture; they sold off their horses, cattle, sheep, farming equipment and fruit trees.

It was at this juncture, in January of 1842, that John Bidwell arrived on Sutter's ranch equipped with a Mexican passport and very little else. Sutter hired him on—at $25 a month—and assigned him to collect the movable assets of his Russian purchase. Bidwell went at the job with a thoroughness that was to become his trademark. Besides sending out the Russians' livestock and equipment, he dismantled their buildings for construction lumber. And since the fruit trees were too big to move, he organized a harvest and sent Sutter quantities of dried fruit and apple cider.

Sutter was impressed with Bidwell's industry and intelligence and made him his bookkeeper and chief lieutenant. In this dual capacity Bidwell learned the techniques and economics of ranching. Soon he was helping manage Sutter's varied operations: cattle, sheep, vegetable gardens, orchards and fields that yielded as much as 40,000 bushels of wheat a year. But Sutter's debts to the Russians and others consumed the profits of his sound operations. Bidwell wrote: "Sutter started many other new enterprises in order to find relief from his embarrassments; but in spite of all he could do, these increased."

Between Sutter's mistakes and his own growing knowledge, Bidwell thought more and more of ranching on his own. His ruminations came to focus one day in 1843 while he was riding up the Sacramento Valley in search of some missing horses. He found himself in lush, beautiful country near Chico Creek. "The plains," he wrote, "were covered with scattered groves of spreading oaks; there were wild grasses and clover, two, three and four feet high, and most luxuri-ant. The fertility of the soil was beyond question, and the waters of Chico Creek were clear, cold and sparkling; the mountains were lovely and flower-covered, a beautiful scene." Here, Bidwell decided, he would locate himself for life.

With Sutter's blessing he left New Helvetia to put his experience to work for himself. Following his mentor's lead, he took out Mexican citizenship and in 1845 obtained his own grant. During the next seven years, through a series of trades and purchases, he acquired 22,000 acres of the land he coveted. Over the course of half a century, John Bidwell's Rancho del Arroyo Chico would earn a reputation as one of the most highly diversified ranching operations in California, and thus the entire West.

When Bidwell occupied his land he built himself a small house and bought a modest starter herd of longhorns. To obtain the finest cuttings for his vineyards and orchards, he saddled up and rode more than 600 miles to the Mission San Luis Rey de Francia near San Diego. He planted his first vines and grains in 1847 and dug what was probably the first irrigation ditch in the Sacramento Valley.

But Bidwell's work of establishing Rancho Chico suffered from several momentous interruptions; in the years between 1844 and 1849 he took part in more history than most men do in a lifetime. Though he was a peace-loving, religious man, Bidwell bore arms in 1844 to help the California governor put down a small-bore revolution. Then Captain John Frémont arrived from the United States with a band of frontiersmen and helped foment a large-caliber rebellion against the government by Americans living in California. This time Bidwell, torn between loyalties, joined the revolt with a mixture of American patriotism and personal distaste, assuming—he later wrote—that Frémont's mission "was simply a pretense to justify the premature beginning of the Mexican War, which henceforth was to be carried on in the name of the United States." When the Mexican War did begin, Bidwell backed the invading American troops with no reservations, and so did John Sutter, always "a warm admirer of the United States."

Hostilities had scarcely ended when California was rocked again by the epoch-making discovery of gold, which Bidwell reverently attributed to "the hand of

Providence." Early in 1848, a few months after the great strike at Sutter's Mill on the south fork of the American River, Bidwell made a sizable strike of his own on the Feather River. He used the gold to buy and stock more land.

Fortunately, Bidwell's ranch property was off the beaten track. While the lands of his friend John Sutter were being trampled, robbed and ruined by hordes of ruthless fortune hunters on their way to gold fields in the Sierra foothills, Bidwell expanded his operation to meet the demand for staples, grain and especially livestock. The scrawny longhorns suddenly became infinitely more valuable for their meat than they had been for their hides. In 1849 the price for beef in the brand-new town of Sacramento reached $500 a head, at least 200 times the price scarcely a year earlier. A decade-long cattle boom was under way.

Feeding the gold rushers was a hectic operation that required the cooperation of two separate ranching societies: the new, fast-growing, hard-driving American communities in the northern interior and the old, static but now galvanized Mexican settlements along the southern coast. Large herds of bawling, milling cattle were driven north by the Mexican ranchers and the few Americans who had joined them; Don Abel Stearns of the Rancho Los Alamitos became a leading figure in the cattle drives to the gold fields and added substantially to his already considerable fortune. As the supply of livestock dwindled in the north and in the south, new herds began arriving from the east, principally from Texas.

But then, flushed with success, nearly all of the California ranchers courted disaster by overexpanding their herds to supply what appeared to be a constant influx of gold seekers. Gold production began to taper off by 1853, and the rush of miners declined with it.

John Bidwell, ever methodical and judicious, did not overexpand his cattle herd; he hewed to his belief in diversification. He laid out and planted additional vineyards and orchards. With a handful of Indian laborers, he tilled the soil with crude wooden plows, planted a good amount of wheat, harvested it with sickles and threshed it by Sutter's method: stampeding horses over it in a round corral.

The gold rush was still at fever pitch when Bidwell's plantings began to bear fruit. In 1851 he was able to send a gift of grapevines and young fruit trees to a friend on a ranch 50 miles away, receiving in return "ten fine hens, well cooped." The next year he built a new house, a two-story structure of baked mud brick that he affectionately called Old Adobe. The next year he built a water-powered mill and made a tidy profit selling flour to newcomers in the valley.

Bidwell continued to innovate. He established the first important experimental farm and nursery in California, seeking better ways to make use of California's climate and soil. Learning horticulture by trial and error, he planted a succession of new and improved varieties of plants, carefully making notes on their culture and maturity dates. He introduced almonds and casaba melons to California, pioneered in the making of olive oil, and raised Chinese sugar cane, Egyptian corn, Italian and Spanish chestnuts. He experimented with varieties of pears, nectarines, quinces, figs, pomegranates and other fruits, sorghum and maize. He also studied viticulture and produced wines, which he offered to his visitors along with Rancho Chico beef, mutton, chicken, turkey, eggs, bread, butter and honey.

Bidwell's career as a wine maker, however, was brief. In 1864 he was elected a United States congressman, and by the end of his two-year term in Washington he had become convinced of the virtues of temperance and the deleterious effects of even the most innocent of wines. Returning home, he uprooted his wine grapes and planted raisin and table grapes in their stead. This done, he spent much of his time supervising the construction of a magnificent new house near the bank of Chico Creek. He had started building the mansion for himself but had since acquired a better reason for wanting it: his bride to be, Annie Kennedy of Washington, D.C.

Bidwell Mansion was finished in 1868, just after Annie's arrival, at the considerable cost of $56,500. It was one of northern California's most celebrated showplaces, a triumph of ornate Victorian architecture surrounded by lawns, flower gardens and a dazzling collection of native and imported trees. Noted men in many fields of endeavor enjoyed Bidwell's hospitality; among them were the eminent botanists Sir Joseph Hooker and Asa Gray, conservationist John Muir (himself a successful fruit rancher near

Rancher-Congressman John Bidwell met Annie Kennedy, a crusading Washington spinster of 27, in 1864. Three years later, through perseverance and a shared enthusiasm for temperance and women's suffrage, he persuaded her to marry him.

Martinez), General William Tecumseh Sherman and President and Mrs. Rutherford B. Hayes.

By the 1880s Rancho Chico resembled a benevolent feudal domain. Much of the steady labor was performed by a band of about 100 Mechoopda Indians, who came to be called "Bidwell's Indians." Bidwell treated them well, paid them decent wages and provided them with dwellings close to the mansion. He considered himself their protector. One day he found a man forcing his attentions on an Indian woman and thrashed him soundly with a willow stick. He nearly paid the highest price for his indignation, narrowly escaping with his life when the man later came after him with a gun.

Despite his towering success as a rancher, Bidwell remained a modest man. If a guest happened to be visiting during the wheat harvest, he would refrain from mentioning that one of his wheat fields was a thousand acres in extent, or that at the Paris Interna-

tional Exposition of 1878 he had won a gold medal for the finest wheat in the world. But he did indulge in one vanity. He would send one of his men out early in the morning to get the first sack of grain from the big harvester, rush it to the mill to have it ground into flour and speed the flour to the mansion's kitchen door. Seated for breakfast, which was served promptly at 8 o'clock, Bidwell would pass to his guest a plate of fresh, steaming muffins and remark with an air of casual triumph, "These biscuits this morning were growing in the field!"

It was a sense of civic responsibility that prompted Bidwell to pursue his political career. Forthright, incorruptible, teetotaling and at times more than a bit prim—his political opponents referred to him as "Sister Bidwell"—he had been elected state senator in 1849. After his four years as U.S. Representative, he was defeated in three campaigns for the California governorship on independent tickets. In 1892 he ran

Flags and climbing roses drape the parlor doorways of John Bidwell's 26-room ranch house *(inset)* in Chico as tea is served in the adjoining dining room. The plants, grown outdoors to Annie Bidwell's specifications, were carried inside for festivities. The flags, each bearing 31 stars, symbolize Bidwell's pride in his role in making California the 31st state in 1850.

as the Prohibition candidate for President of the United States; again he lost, but he polled the largest number of votes ever recorded by that party.

In his seventies Bidwell retired from politics to give his time to his ranch and to crusading for irrigation, flood control and water conservation. Repeatedly he spoke out for his guiding principle: diversification. "Agriculture," he argued, "must be better and more varied, to embrace everything within the range of our unequaled and diversified soil and climate."

Bidwell was still at work when he was stricken one day while sawing cottonwood logs and died, at the age of 80, in the year 1900.

Through Bidwell's long career, other ranchers less moral than he were pursuing a more hard-eyed, spectacular vision of empire. In California there existed a real chance for land monopoly, and a few shrewd, powerful men came close to making the possibility a reality. Their opportunity had been created by Mexico's casual system of land grants.

Before the United States took possession of California in 1846, the Mexican government had awarded huge grants of the best land to native Californians and to a small number of American immigrants. That, in itself, was verging on monopoly, for only 39 million of California's 102 million acres were tillable. As American newcomers began arriving in substantial numbers, they found only one million acres of the granted land in use, given over mostly to scrawny cattle and primitive agriculture. To them this situation seemed both undemocratic and inefficient, and they demanded a more equitable distribution of land. The United States authorities heeded their cries.

There were other reasons for taking action as well. Treaty terms with Mexico bound the United States to respect previously issued grants. But many of the land titles — particularly those awarded in a flurry just before the war — were of such dubious authenticity that in 1851 a land act was passed setting up a commission to review individual claims. In all, 813 claims to a total of 13 million acres were heard by the commission over the next four years. Nearly 300 were rejected as fraudulent, dismissed for technical reasons or withdrawn. Even the 521 that were confirmed remained in dispute by counterclaimants and

ranch. Wheat growers in sparsely manned California welcomed the laborsaving harvesters after they were perfected in the mid-1870s.

From imported vines, a bonanza of wine grapes

"Vine-planting is like the beginning of mining for precious metals," wrote Robert Louis Stevenson after visiting California vineyards during the early 1880s. "The wine-grower also 'prospects.' One corner of the land after another is tried with one kind of grape after another."

The first grape tried in California was the Mission variety, so named because it was brought from Mexico by Franciscan padres during the 18th Century and cultivated in their missions for sacramental wine. In 1824 an American, Joseph Chapman, first planted Mission grapevines for commercial purposes, choosing fertile land near Los Angeles.

But it was an immigrant grape rancher, aptly named Vignes (meaning vines in French) and born in the wine region of Bordeaux, who first

"prospected" for a better grape. In 1831 he imported French cuttings to improve his Southern vineyard.

The most relentless seeker after better grapes and better land was a Hungarian aristocrat, Agoston Haraszthy. A political refugee from Hungary in 1840, he sent for cuttings from his family's vineyards on the Danube. In America Haraszthy transplanted himself and his vines several times to find the ideal soil and terrain. From Wisconsin he migrated to San Diego's Mission Valley, then up the coast to San Francisco, then down to San Mateo County. Finally, in 1857, Haraszthy found what he was looking for. In the hills of Sonoma County he tasted a Mission vintage so impressive that he decided this was the right place to put down his cuttings of zinfandel, feher szagos,

flame tokay and many other varieties.

He did more than just plant. He also exhorted his fellow growers to set out their vines on high, gravely, unirrigated ground with good drainage. By 1860 Haraszthy's success as a vintner, as well as his zeal for improving the product, prompted the state to send him on a vine-collecting expedition to the great vineyards of Europe. He returned the next year with 100,000 plants of almost 300 varieties and distributed cuttings to growers all over California.

Agoston Haraszthy's prospecting enriched the state incalculably. Due largely to his work, the production of California wine leaped from 58,000 gallons in 1850 to three million gallons in 1870. As a matter of fact, the old grape prospector had struck a vein of gold that would never run out.

Workers disgorge the sediment, perfect the fill and recork champagne bottles at Haraszthy's Sonoma vineyard in the early 1870s.

challenges to boundary surveys. The net result was that ownership of much of California's best land remained in doubt for years. Many would-be settlers grew so tired of waiting for good land to be cleared for claim that they went back to the East or moved to other Western territories.

Some of the claims rejected by the commission were transparent fakes, but a few were drawn skillfully enough to frighten legitimate owners. A shameless rake named José Limantour, once a merchant in Monterey, produced convincing-looking papers purporting that he had been given 530,000 acres—including most of the city of San Francisco—and he very nearly got away with his bold scheme. Only through the detective work of United States Attorney Edwin M. Stanton, later Secretary of War under President Lincoln, were the documents proved to have been cleverly forged and antedated. As Stanton developed the case against the sometime trader, Limantour's lawyers abandoned him and the schemer himself beat a hasty retreat to an unannounced destination. Attorney General Jeremiah Black, who was Stanton's superior, sweepingly pronounced Limantour's claim to be "the most stupendous fraud ever perpetrated in the history of the world."

Of the genuine claims, most were not specifically located or developed. Others were improperly registered and had boundaries that were overlapping or bewilderingly vague. Some were so-called floating grants, which permitted the grantees, or their heirs, to scatter their allocated acreage throughout areas five or 10 times as large as the size of the grant itself. The claimants could then survey the final boundaries so as to include all the best pieces of land in the area, just as long as the boundaries of each piece touched one another. These floaters were carefully laid out in all sorts of fantastic, gerrymandered shapes in order to pre-empt water sources, other settlers' improvements and even, in one case, a working gold mine; one claim was described as looking "like a tarantula" on the map. Until such a claim was finally located and the boundaries legally defined by the land commission, it was impossible to determine where the grant ended and public lands began.

By an act of 1852 the state of California further complicated the situation by authorizing the sale of inexpensive scrip, or land coupons, which could be used to acquire public land even before any legitimate surveys had separated such land from the ill-defined claims. Given the cloudy land titles and the opportunities for buying up piles of cheap paper and converting it into land, it was not difficult for individuals with a little ingenuity and capital to acquire vast amounts of acreage. A number of smooth operators pulled off dazzling coups within the letter of the law or just a little outside of it. But all their endeavors paled beside the tireless, methodical, often extralegal land acquisitions of California's super-rancher, Henry Miller.

At the zenith of his career around the turn of the century, Miller had accumulated about a million acres of California land, plus vast holdings in Nevada and Oregon, and he controlled, through lease and grazing arrangements, probably ten times more land than that. It was said—with some exaggeration—that he could travel from Oregon to the Mexican border and sleep on his own land every night.

This talented buccaneer was born not Henry Miller but Heinrich Alfred Kreiser, the son of a butcher in the little German village of Brackenheim, not far from Heidelberg. A determined lad with a large head, powerful shoulders and short stubby legs, he scurried around the countryside buying up livestock for his father and tending herds in the family pasture. By the age of 15 he knew every aspect of the meat business, from raising stock to slaughtering and marketing it. He also possessed an elephantine memory, an extraordinary knack for figures and a decided impatience with school and home. In 1844, at the age of 17, he bundled up his few possessions and made his way to Holland, then to England and finally to New York. There he got a job, working 16 hours a day as a pork butcher for eight dollars a month.

While in New York he struck up an acquaintance with a young shoe salesman named Henry Miller who had bought passage on a ship to California to join the gold rush but at the last minute decided not to go. The butcher boy, sniffing opportunity, talked his friend into selling him the ticket at a bargain rate. As he was boarding the ship under the purser's eye he noticed belatedly that the ticket was made out to "Henry Miller" and stamped "not transferable." Heinrich Kreiser became Henry Miller on the spot.

Eight years later, by then highly influential, he had the California state legislature pass a special bill legalizing his adopted name.

When Henry Miller arrived in San Francisco in 1850 he had exactly six dollars in his pocket. He found his way to a fly-ridden lean-to that passed for a butcher shop and approached the man lounging in front of it. The only account of what happened comes down to us complete with accent; a listener recorded it just as Miller later told it. "I just come on the poat," Miller said. "I'm a putcher, and wants a chob." The man told him that he had no job for "putchers." "I knew he was making fun of my English," Miller recalled, "so I then goes down the street and sees a sign 'Dishwasher Wanted.' I takes the chob."

Miller washed dishes for a few days, then found work with an Irish butcher. The following year he saw a chance to open up a butcher shop of his own. In the evenings he hung around saloons where cattle dealers gathered, never drinking but always eavesdropping unabashedly to pick up information about available animals and prices. Invariably, he was the first man at the stockyards the next morning to get the pick of the meat. He had been in business only two years when he had saved enough money to buy a herd of 300 cattle for $33,000. The animals were not lanky longhorns but one of the first herds of heftier Eastern cattle to reach California.

As Miller acquired more beef on the hoof, he began to look around for land to graze them on. On a trip down the San Joaquin Valley he came on a ranch owned by two brothers named Hildreth and bought from them 8,835 acres at $1.15 an acre, along with 7,500 head of cattle at five dollars a head and the brothers' "HH" brand. In 1858 he formed a partnership with his leading competitor in the meat business, an Alsatian immigrant named Charles Lux, thus eliminating an annoying rival and finding a useful ally who could handle the city end of the business while he looked for new opportunities in the field.

Miller launched a campaign of land buying that was to last for more than 30 years. He bought land for specific uses and also, as he told a real estate agent, for investment. When the agent suggested that he no longer needed the old lot in San Francisco where he had first set up his butcher shop, Henry Miller replied, "Land in California is cheap now; it will be valuable. Wise men buy land; fools sell."

At first Miller bought or leased small ranch properties, spaced apart at convenient intervals so he could move his cattle about to the best pastures, feeding and fattening them along the way from range to market. Gradually he expanded onto adjacent lands as the herds bearing the Double-H brand increased. He bought so quietly and moved on so quickly that for a few years his campaign attracted little notice. Then ranchers suddenly woke up to the fact that a German butcher named Miller owned or controlled half a million acres of California, and in one place had put up a fence 68 miles long.

Miller got his land in a variety of licit and illicit ways. He speculated in scrip, acquiring more than 180,000 acres of former public lands at well under a dollar an acre. He would search out one or a few — but not all — of the heirs to a Mexican land grant and buy their interests cheaply, obtaining the right to range his cattle over the entire grant. Gradually he would assume sole practical control and force the rest of the heirs to sell at his price. He bought out bankrupt farmers; he made loans to smaller ranchers and when they fell on hard times, foreclosed and took over their lands, their stock, their houses and barns. He also showed considerable skill in breaking homestead laws — since a man could claim only one homestead of limited acreage from the public domain, then had to build a house and live there to prove his claim, Miller hired dummy claimants to do the dirty work for him, thus prying away additional chunks of public land.

Miller realized that water was more important to California's future than gold, and he not only sought out naturally irrigated land for his crop and pasture land but made elaborate plans to assure himself a steady artificial supply. To control the precious water, he acquired property on both sides of the San Joaquin River for a stretch of more than 120 miles and built levees and irrigation ditches for a distance of 50 miles. He also watched with great interest the formation of the San Joaquin and Kings River Canal Company, which planned to irrigate a vast area of the valley.

Miller invoked the common-law doctrine of riparian rights — which held that the owner of land located along a watercourse had the right to have the water

Rancher John Sutter was almost bankrupt before the gold rush ruined him. Kindhearted to a fault, he hired all comers, created useless jobs for them and, said an aide, put himself "almost hopelessly in debt."

estates was good news to men on the lookout for small- and medium-size ranches.

In practice, however, each of these gains had a problematical side. Farming required many more workers than cattle raising, and the accelerated shift to crops created a seasonal labor shortage. Moreover, the high cost of effective irrigation worked to the disadvantage of small ranchers, tending to preserve—and even to expand—the huge land holdings of wealthy ranchers in the north who could afford to crosshatch their acreage with irrigation ditches.

The livestock crisis taught California ranchers one lesson that was all to the good—a lesson that the big cattlemen of the Great Plains learned to their dismay a quarter century later: sheep were the safest and most profitable livestock investment. Sheep needed less water than cattle, less care than cattle and less grazing land, for they cropped grass right down to ground level instead of nibbling off the tops as cattle did. Best of all, sheep flourished in upland pastures unsuitable for large-scale farming and thus added millions of productive acres to California's supply of useful land.

Sheep ranching increased in California even more dramatically than cattle raising declined. Like the cattle herds of the gold-rush days, sheep flocks had been practically wiped out by heavy consumption, then replenished with imports from New Mexico and elsewhere. In 1860 the state counted around one million woollies; then the California ranchers took over and worked wonders.

Within two decades, the state's sheep population had soared to an estimated 7.7 million. Moreover, the quality of the flocks had increased apace with the quantity; the original Mexican *churro* stock—small, coarse-coated animals—were rapidly improved by crossbreeding with heftier, finer-coated imports from the East and Europe. As early as 1861 a traveling reporter for a stockmen's journal discovered that many progressive ranchers were already well advanced in the upgrading campaign. Of the 3,300 sheep owned by two partners near Los Angeles, the reporter noted that "about 1,500 are Merinos, and Saxons. The balance of the flock are American Cotswold, Southdown and crosses. The wool is of fine quality, many of the sheep having sheared over 12 pounds each. The last crop of wool was over 10,000 pounds."

Before long the *churro* strain was practically eliminated by crossbreeding.

Many Californians prospered on ranches devoted solely to sheep. Paradoxically, one of the biggest sheep specialists was so famous for his colorful non-ranching career that people outside of California thought of him as everything but a rancher. His name was Edward Fitzgerald Beale. He started sheep ranching in the inland hills of southern California in the 1850s, buying huge chunks of real estate from absentee Mexican owners for an average of five cents an acre. Two decades later, his Rancho El Tejon, named after an abandoned Mexican fort on the land, totaled 300,000 acres and boasted 125,000 sheep.

"Ned" Beale had come to California in 1846 as a 24-year-old naval officer in the American invasion force. He first attracted notice in the key battle of San

Rancher Ned Beale won fame from two sensational journeys. Disguised as a *vaquero (left)* in 1848, he dashed through hostile Mexico carrying California gold-strike news to Washington. Then in 1857, when the Army was testing camels *(below)* for desert use, Beale took the beasts on an astonishing 3,000-mile trek through the Southwest.

Pascuale when he stole through the lines of encircling Mexican soldiers to bring reinforcements from San Diego, some 50 miles away. Beale topped that feat in 1848 by making a sensational dash from California to Washington, D.C., with the first official news of the gold strike at Sutter's Mill. Instead of traveling directly overland, Beale decided it would be faster to head south to Mexico. He raced on horseback through the bandit-infested Mexican wilds to Veracruz, from there by sloop and later by stagecoach to deliver his message—and a sample of gold dust—to the State Department. His 4,000-mile journey took him 47 days, a remarkable pace for that time of slow travel.

More bravura followed. While exploring the Southwest in the 1850s, Beale conceived the notion that camels could solve the Army's problem of transportation in Western deserts. He and a few others bombarded the War Department with persuasive arguments in favor of a camel experiment. The result was a memorable Western curiosity: 77 "ships of the desert" were imported from Tunis and established as the United States Army's Camel Corps.

In 1857 Beale was assigned to take the camels on a dry run from Texas to California. He left from San Antonio, and at El Paso he sent an enthusiastic letter to the Secretary of War praising his charges. "They are the most docile, patient and easily managed creatures in the world and infinitely more workable than mules," he wrote. Also, he discovered, they could carry 700-pound packs, thrive at a temperature of 104° and flourish on a diet of greasewood shrubs. Six months later, Beale and his caravan arrived in Los Angeles and dumfounded the citizens with a leisurely parade through the city streets. A newspaperman who witnessed the spectacle told the world that the camels could go without water for six to 10 days and declared, on their drivers' authority, that "they will get fat where a jackass would starve to death."

At this point, however, everyone but Beale lost interest in the beasts. Nothing came of the successful experiment, and during the Civil War most of the camels wandered off into the deserts of Arizona and New Mexico, startling Indians, settlers and passersby. Beale, overcome with sympathy for the neglected camels, bought them from the Army and retired them to his ranch. After a while, his neighbors got used to seeing him on his periodic 100-mile excursions from his ranch to Los Angeles, sitting in a sulky drawn by two camels in tandem, conversing with them in Syrian, which he had taught himself on the whimsical theory that it was their native tongue.

Beale periodically left his ranch on government assignments; he served as California's surveyor general, as superintendent of Indian affairs in the state, even as U.S. minister to Austria-Hungary. But in his absence his superb chief herder, José Jésus Lopez, kept his huge sheep herds growing. Journalist Charles Nordhoff, visiting Rancho El Tejon in 1872, was awed by the vastness of the spread. "You may ride for eighty miles on the county road upon this great estate," he wrote. "It supports this year over one hundred thousand sheep." The sheep were herded in bands of 1,300 to 2,000 and corralled near water every night; in the morning a supply train of mules and donkeys would be sent out with food for the distant herders. "Eight or nine weeks," Nordhoff noted, "are required to shear the whole flock." Beale annually marketed 175,000 pounds of wool.

For all its size, the Rancho El Tejon could not support Beale's enormous sheep population the whole year round, and he had to make use of a million mountainous acres of the public domain. Like other ranchers in the sheep towns that sprang up around Bakersfield, Beale sent his herders and their flocks on a long annual route. Each spring, after the sheep had grazed the lowlands until the grasses dried out, the solitary herders headed north through Owens Valley onto the eastern slopes of the Sierra Nevada, each man going to his chosen upland pastures. Come autumn, all the herders started their flocks homeward,

often traveling on the gentler western slopes of the mountain range, through the San Joaquin foothills and either the Kings River area or the Kern Valley.

While they wandered along their traditional routes, Beale's herders saw nothing of him, and they had little to do with him once they returned to Rancho El Tejon. Yet, apparently, Beale was to them a trusted friend and admired leader rather than a mere employer; the quiet, deep feeling that his closest workers had for him was perhaps a better measure of the man than the flowery newspaper tributes that announced Ned Beale's death in 1893. Told of his friend's passing, an aged Indian who had traveled with Beale for many years said, "I do not care to live any longer." A day later the Indian died too.

After peaking in the 1870s, California's sheep population declined, due in no small degree to heavy exports that were stocking new ranches in the Great Plains. Even so, sheep ranching remained relatively stable compared with the waves of change that rippled across California's rich, hot lowlands.

In the San Joaquin and Sacramento valleys a mania for wheat gripped the countryside after the flood and drought of the early 1860s. Wheat had proved to be an easy and highly profitable way of using large blocks of land. In rich new soils, with normal rainfall, an acre would yield 30 or 40 bushels of wheat worth $1.50 or more per bushel when the market was good. A yield of 50 bushels per acre was not uncommon, and in a few exceptional cases ranchers brought in 80 bushels per acre from their best land.

Wheat output skyrocketed. In 1873 California became the nation's biggest wheat-producing state and stayed in or close to the lead through the decade. "Wheat, wheat, wheat," exclaimed journalist Nordhoff, traveling between Stockton and Merced in the early 1870s, "nothing but wheat as far as the eye can reach over the plain in every direction. Fields of two, three and four thousand acres make but small farms; here is a man who 'has in' 20,000 acres; here one with 40,000 acres, and another with some still more preposterous amount—all in wheat."

Wheat production declined thereafter. But the wheat craze was supplanted by an even headier boom in other crops. As irrigated areas expanded and new feeder lines provided direct connections to the transcontinental railroads, many ranchers turned to raising perishable fruits and vegetables for Eastern markets. California by 1899 was the nation's biggest producer of grapes and several orchard fruits. Enormous freight-car loads of oranges, lemons, limes and other fruits were shipped out and distributed from coast to coast. On dinner tables in Chicago, Boston, Philadelphia and New York, more and more glasses were filled with California wines.

Everything about California—its wheat and sheep, its grapes and oranges, its clear air and the sunlight on its tawny hills—seemed to be made of purest gold. These assets, talked up by casual visitors as well as by professional publicists, attracted the very rich and the very poor, the robust and the wheezy asthmatic. People from everywhere dreamed of moving West and settling in California on their own "rancho," even if it were only a few acres, even if its cash crop were only chickens or table grapes. Many were drawn to southern California, which in the 1870s and 1880s experienced a land rush that outstripped the gold rush; the state's population more than doubled in that period, reaching 1.2 million in 1890. Real estate promoters ballyhooed the fertility of the soil and hawked lots with such zeal and hyperbole that by 1890 cynical Easterners were sure that all the southern Californians could do was to "irrigate, cultivate and exaggerate." Most exaggerated of all were the boosters' claims for the climate, which they guaranteed would banish all mortal ills. Said one promoter, when customers balked at paying inflated prices for lots of dubious worth: "Hell, we're selling the *climate!* We're *throwing in* the land!"

The popular notion of the California ranch as a vast fiefdom ruled by a shrewd but kindly aristocrat began to fade as the new arrivals cleared their small plots, milked cows, planted orange trees, built beehives, bottled honey and wine. Between 1880 and 1900 the number of California ranches doubled and the average ranch's size was reduced from 462 to 397 acres. Everyone who wanted a small piece of paradise could now have it, if he could afford it.

But many great ranches remained great. Some did break up on the death of their pioneer founders, but new ones were formed by faceless corporations. As an institution, the huge California ranch had led Western agriculture into the age of big business, and it seemed destined to survive for one reason that was hard to dispute. In intensive farming great size usually made for great efficiency; large ranches realized operating economies and profits that were beyond the reach of small and even medium-size ranches.

The persistence of the big California ranches stood out in sharp contrast to the continuing failure of even larger cattle ranches elsewhere in the Old West. Those giants had been breaking up ever since the cruel winter of 1886-1887, when tens of thousands of cattle had frozen or starved to death on overgrazed ranch lands. At the turn of the century, the biggest cattle spread of them all, the 3,000,000-acre XIT Ranch in Texas, was beginning to break up, its owners selling off great chunks of land to cattlemen, to farmers and to real estate developers, who in turn broke down their tracts into townships.

The facts of life in the giant Western cattle industry had become quite clear: great ranch size did not make for great efficiency. On the contrary, it made operations harder, more costly and less profitable. The few big cattle spreads that stayed in business on the Great Plains, most notably the 600,000-acre King Ranch in Texas, survived in spite of their size not because of it. The new, compact, efficient cattle ranches, raising improved herds of heavier cattle on less acreage, were making the business sounder and more profitable than the pioneer cattlemen had ever dreamed before the beef boom went bust.

California ranching was unique, thanks largely to the state's unique combination of fertile soil and mild climate. California was, as its pioneer historian Hubert Howe Bancroft stated at an early date, the place for "a final display of what man can do at his best." But the Great Plains, developing in a different way on a different timetable, was also such a place. Its pioneer ranchers, too, had shown what men could do in the face of adversity. And if veteran cattlemen in Texas or Kansas were saddened to see sodbusters planting crops where longhorns once grazed, they had plenty of consolation and cause for pride: it had been up to these men to open new territories for settlement. The advance of farms, towns and great cities was testimony to the historic contribution of the pioneering ranchers.

Romantic visions of a world on the wane

By 1870 California cattle ranching was giving way to more profitable endeavors. Yet ranchers were largely responsible for preserving the cattleman's way of life. They were generous patrons to a number of wandering artists, giving them food and shelter for weeks. In return the painters enriched the ranchers—and posterity—with a vivid record of the industry that opened most of the West for settlers.

The master painters of California ranch life were German-born William Hahn and English-born James Walker, who toured the West Coast Eden in the 1870s. Walker's action-packed paintings of the cowboys' work helped make them a symbol of independence and adventure to city-bound gallerygoers in the East. Hahn, smitten by California's sun-soaked landscape, painted scenes of both stock raising and farming, which became inseparable as the great open country developed. Thus, in painting California ranch life, the two artists also summed up half a century of progress in the West.

224

Two cowboys prepare to slaughter a steer at Rancho Santa Margarita, where the artist James Walker sojourned on his California tour.

Twirling lariats, cowboys head off runaway horses in a roundup scene painted by James Walker at the Mission de San Fernando Rancho. Named after a nearby mission where local stock raising began in 1797, the ranch became one of California's leading breeders of horses and cattle.

227

Astride a white horse, rancher Jaime del Valle arbitrates a cattle dispute between two neighbors in the Santa Clarita Valley. The painting, done by James Walker, paid tribute to the esteemed judge whose impromptu hearings at trouble spots often settled arguments without any violence.

Pausing on a trail drive, cowboys are plied with refreshment in William Hahn's painting of a Monterey ranch scene. California ranchers were proverbially hospitable, a tradition dating back to Spanish times. Many a newcomer conducted his journey on a series of horses, borrowing a steed at one ranch and then leaving it at the next.

In William Hahn's *Harvest Time, Sacramento Valley*, ranch hands bring wheat to a threshing rig turned by horses, then bag the grain and load it on a wagon. As California ranchers shifted from raising stock to growing crops, they wrung wealth without precedent from their fertile lands.

TEXT CREDITS

For full reference of specific page credits see bibliography

Chapter I: Particularly useful sources for information and quotes in this chapter: Lewis Atherton, *The Cattle Kings,* University of Nebraska Press, 1972; J. Frank Dobie, *The Mustangs,* Little, Brown and Company, 1952; Tom Lea, *The King Ranch,* Little, Brown and Company, 1957; Lewis Nordyke, *Great Roundup,* William Morrow & Co., 1955; 7—description of ranchers, Roosevelt, *Ranch Life in the Far West,* p. 6. Chapter II: Particularly useful sources: E. C. Abbott and Helena Huntington Smith, *We Pointed Them North,* University of Nebraska Press, 1942; John Albright, "Historic Resource Study and Historic Structure Report, Historical Data, Grant-Kohrs National Historic Site, Montana," (unpublished manuscript); Robert H. Fletcher, *Free Grass to Fences,* University Publishers Incorporated, 1960; Michael S. Kennedy, ed., *Cowboys and Cattlemen,* Hastings House, Publishers, 1964; Granville Stuart, *Forty Years on the Frontier as Seen in the Journals and Reminiscences of Granville Stuart,* edited by Paul C. Phillips, The Arthur H. Clark Company, 1925; Paul Robert Treece, "Mr. Montana: The Life of Granville Stuart, 1834-1918," (unpublished doctoral dissertation, Ohio State University, 1974); 55—road ranchers, Mattes, p. 270. Chapter III: Particularly useful sources: Howard Louis Conard, *Uncle Dick Wootton,* edited by Milo Milton Quaife, The Lakeside Press, 1957; Archer B. Gilfillan, *Sheep,* Little, Brown and Company, 1930; Winifred Kupper, *The Golden Hoof,* Alfred A. Knopf, Inc., 1945; Robert Laxalt, "Basque Sheepherders," *National Geographic,* Vol. 129, No. 6, June 1966; Willard Leonard, "A Boyhood with Sheep in the Oregon Desert," *Oregon Historical Quarterly,* Vol. 76, No. 4, December 1975; Robert Maudslay, *Texas Sheepman,* edited by Winifred Kupper, Books for Libraries Press, 1971; Charles Wayland Towne and Edward Norris Wentworth, *Shepherd's Empire,* University of Oklahoma Press, 1945; Edward Norris Wentworth,

America's Sheep Trails, Iowa State College Press, 1948; 103—Basques, Douglass and Bilbao, pp. 274, 270. Chapter IV: Particularly useful sources: Mark Brown, *The Plainsmen of the Yellowstone,* University of Nebraska Press, 1961; David H. Grover, *Diamondfield Jack,* University of Nevada Press, 1968; Kupper, *The Golden Hoof;* Wentworth, *America's Sheep Trails;* Clara T. Woody and Milton L. Schwartz, *Globe, Arizona,* Arizona Historical Society, 1977; 112—resolution, Fletcher, p. 50. Chapter V: Particularly useful sources: Donald Dresden, *The Marquis de Morès,* University of Oklahoma Press, 1970; Hermann Hagedorn, *Roosevelt in the Bad Lands,* Houghton Mifflin Company, 1921; Carleton Putnam, *Theodore Roosevelt,* Vol. I, Charles Scribner's Sons, 1958; Theodore Roosevelt, *The Autobiography of Theodore Roosevelt,* edited by Wayne Andrews, Octagon Books, 1975; Marshall Sprague, *A Gallery of Dudes,* Little, Brown and Company, 1967; D. Jerome Tweton, *The Marquis de Morès,* North Dakota Institute for Regional Studies, 1972; 158—description of the West, Brisbin, p. 5; 176—Sewall quote, Sewall, p. 27. Chapter VI: Particularly useful sources: John Bidwell, *Echoes of the Past,* Arno Press, 1973; Stephen Bonsal, *Edward Fitzgerald Beale,* G. P. Putnam's Sons, 1912; Paul W. Gates, *California Ranchos and Farms,* The State Historical Society of Wisconsin, 1967; Rockwell D. Hunt, *John Bidwell,* Caxton Printers, Ltd., 1942; Bernard Taper, "The King of Ranchers," *American Heritage,* Vol. 18, No. 5, August 1967; Edward F. Treadwell, *The Cattle King,* Valley Publishers, 1950; 210—prospecting analogy, Stevenson, p. 2; 214—seasonal reminders, Miller manuscript, Clay quote, Clay, p. 28; 218—Miller's political clout, McWilliams, *Factories in the Field,* p. 35; 219—grasshopper invasion, Cleland, p. 126; 222—wheat fields, Nordhoff, p. 182.

PICTURE CREDITS

The sources for the illustrations in this book are shown below. Credits from left to right are separated by semicolons, from top to bottom by dashes.

Cover—Linda Lorenz, courtesy Amon Carter Museum, Fort Worth. 2—San Antonio Museum Association, Witte Memorial Museum, San Antonio, Texas. 6,7—Courtesy Montana Historical Society, Helena. 8,9—Courtesy Walter Ferguson Collection, Western History Collections, University of Oklahoma Library. 10,11—Courtesy David R. Phillips Collection. 12,13—Courtesy Western History Research Center, University of Wyoming. 14 through 17—From the Erwin E. Smith Collection of Range Photographs, Library of Congress. 18—Paulus Leeser, courtesy the King Ranch, Inc. 20,21—Bill Malone, courtesy Texas State Archives. 23—Paulus Leeser, courtesy Mrs. J. D. Patch (2). 24,25—Paulus Leeser, courtesy the King Ranch, Inc. (2). 28,29—Courtesy California Historical Society. 31—Courtesy Library of Congress. 32,33—Paulus Leeser, courtesy the King Ranch, Inc.; courtesy San Antonio Museum Association, Witte Memorial Museum. 34—A. A. Forbes, courtesy N. H. Rose Collection, Western History Collections, University of Oklahoma Library. 35—Bill Malone, courtesy Texas State Archives. 38,39,41—Paulus Leeser, courtesy the King Ranch, Inc. 42 through 45—Courtesy Kansas State Historical Society, Topeka. 46,47—Courtesy Library of Congress. 48 through 51—Herb Orth, courtesy Picture Col-

lection, the branch libraries, the New York Public Library. 52,53—Courtesy the Thomas Gilcrease Institute of American History and Art, Tulsa, Oklahoma. 54—Courtesy Montana Historical Society, Helena. 56,57—Courtesy Coffrin's Old West Gallery, photograph by L. A. Huffman, Miles City, Montana. 59 through 63—Courtesy Montana Historical Society, Helena. 64,65—Linda Lorenz, courtesy Amon Carter Museum, Fort Worth. 67—Courtesy Museum of Fine Arts, Boston, from the M. and M. Karolik Collection. 71,72—Courtesy Montana Historical Society, Helena. 73—Courtesy Western History Research Center, University of Wyoming. 74,75—Courtesy State Historical Society of Missouri, Columbia, except inset, top right, courtesy Denver Public Library, Western History Department. 76,77—Courtesy Denver Public Library, Western History Department. 78 through 81—David F. Barry, courtesy Denver Public Library, Western History Department. 82,83—Courtesy Denver Public Library, Western History Department. 84,85—Courtesy Western History Research Center, University of Wyoming. 86—Courtesy Moorhouse Collection, University of Oregon Library. 89—Courtesy Library of Congress. 90—Courtesy Bureau of Indian Affairs, Department of Interior. 91,92,93—Courtesy Library of Congress. 95—

Courtesy Coffrin's Old West Gallery, photograph by L. A. Huffman, Miles City, Montana. 96—Courtesy Western History Research Center, University of Wyoming—William MacWilliam. 97—Courtesy Coffrin's Old West Gallery, photograph by L. A. Huffman, Miles City, Montana—courtesy Arizona Historical Society. 99—Courtesy Coffrin's Old West Gallery, photograph by L. A. Huffman, Miles City, Montana. 100,101—Courtesy Montana Historical Society, Helena. 103—Courtesy Basque Studies Program, University of Nevada, Reno, on loan from Nevada Historical Society. 104,105—Courtesy Oregon Historical Society. 106—Courtesy Denver Public Library, Western History Department. 108—Courtesy A. A. Forbes Collection, Western History Collections, University of Oklahoma Library, except inset, bottom right, courtesy Panhandle-Plains Historical Museum, Canyon, Texas. 110,111—Courtesy Montana Historical Society, Helena. 112,113—Courtesy Denver Public Library, Western History Department. 114—Courtesy Arizona Historical Society. 117—Courtesy National Archives and Records Service (2). 118,119—Courtesy University of Arizona Museum of Art. 120,121—Courtesy Nevada Historical Society, Reno. 122—Courtesy Library of Congress. 126—Courtesy Historical Research and Publications Division, Wyoming State Archives and Historical Department. 128,129—Jim Olive, courtesy the Museum of Texas Tech University-Ranching Heritage Center; courtesy Northern Illinois University Archives—Charles Phillips, courtesy Ellwood House Museum. 130,131—Charles Phillips, courtesy Ellwood House Museum, except inset, top right, courtesy New-York Historical Society, New York City, from the Bella C. Landauer Collection. 132 through 141—Courtesy Arizona Historical Society. 142,143—Courtesy Archives and Manuscripts, Harold B. Lee Library, Brigham Young University. 144 through 149—Courtesy Solomon D. Butcher Collection, Nebraska State Historical Society. 150,151—Courtesy Archives and Manuscripts, Harold B. Lee Library, Brigham Young University. 152,153—Courtesy Theodore Roosevelt Collection, Harvard Col-

lege Library. 154,156,157—Courtesy Denver Public Library, Western History Department. 159—Courtesy Picture Collection of the State Historical Society of North Dakota (3). 160—Benschneider, courtesy De Morès Historic Site. 162—Courtesy Coffrin's Old West Gallery, photograph by L. A. Huffman, Miles City, Montana—Benschneider, courtesy De Morès Historic Site. 164,165—Courtesy Picture Collection of the State Historical Society of North Dakota. 167—Courtesy Denver Public Library, Western History Department. 168,169—Courtesy Coffrin's Old West Gallery, photograph by L. A. Huffman, Miles City, Montana. 173,174,175—Paulus Leeser, courtesy Theodore Roosevelt Birthplace National Historic Site. 178,179—Courtesy Library of Congress, except inset, top right, courtesy Western History Research Center, University of Wyoming. 180 through 187—Emory J. Anderson, courtesy Eatons' Ranch, Wolf, Wyoming. 188 through 195—Courtesy Library of Congress. 196—Courtesy Bancroft Library. 199—Courtesy Huntington Library, San Marino, California. 200,201—Courtesy Bancroft Library. 202—Courtesy Huntington Library, San Marino, California. 205—Courtesy California State Library; courtesy California Historical Society Library. 206,207—Tom Tracy, Historic Photo Collection, courtesy Bidwell Mansion, State Historic Park (2). 208,209—Courtesy California State Library. 210—Courtesy Bancroft Library. 213—Courtesy State Museum, Solethurn, Switzerland. 215,216,217—Ted Streshinsky, courtesy Ralph L. Milliken Museum, Los Banos, California (2). 219—Courtesy California State Library. 220,221—Henry Beville, courtesy Decatur House, a property of the National Trust for Historic Preservation (2). 224,225—Courtesy Bancroft Library. 226 through 229—Wolf von dem Bussche, courtesy Carl S. Dentzel, Los Angeles, California. 230,231—Courtesy Collection of The Oakland Museum, gift of Mr. and Mrs. Sidney L. Schwartz, to honor Dr. and Mrs. John J. Sampson and in memory of Mr. and Mrs. William E. Gump. 232,233—Courtesy Fine Arts Museums of San Francisco, gift of Mrs. Harold McKinnon and Mrs. Harry L. Brown.

ACKNOWLEDGMENTS

The index for this book was prepared by Gale Partoyan and Peter Del Valle. The editors give special thanks to Robert Laxalt, Director, University of Nevada Press, Reno; Holland McCombs, Dallas, Texas; Dr. Rodman Paul, Edward S. Harkness, Professor of History, California Institute of Technology, Pasadena; Carl L. Sonnichsen, Senior Editor, *Journal of Arizona History,* Arizona Historical Society, Tucson; Dr. Paul Treece, Assistant Dean, Central Ohio Technical College, Newark; and Dr. D. Jerome Tweton, Chairman, Department of History, University of North Dakota, Grand Forks, who read and commented on portions of this text. The editors also thank: John Albright, Historian, National Park Service, Denver, Colorado; Marjorie Arkelian, Art Department Historian, Charles Lokey, Curatorial Assistant, George Neubert, Curator of Art, The Oakland Museum, Oakland, California; Richard C. Bailey, Director, Kern County Museum, Bakersfield, California; Margaret Bret Harte, Head Librarian, Susan Peters, Reference Librarian, Arizona Historical Society, Tucson; Glenn Britton, Market Analyst, Topper Thorpe, Manager, Cattle-Fax, Denver, Colorado; Mark Brown, Alta, Iowa; Laura Bullion, Director of Library Services, Daniel Bazán, Library Assistant, Institute of Texan Cultures, University of Texas, San Antonio; John Carter, Cura-

tor of Photography, Nebraska State Historical Society, Lincoln; Marion Cook, Price, Utah; Stanley Crane, Librarian, Pequot Library, Southport, Connecticut; John A. Cypher Jr., Assistant to the President, L. A. Walker Jr., Manager of the Henrietta Memorial, King Ranch Inc., Kingsville, Texas; Wallace Dailey, Curator, Theodore Roosevelt Collection, Harvard College Library, Cambridge, Massachusetts; Thomas De Claire, Reference Librarian, Geography and Map Division, Library of Congress, Alexandria; Dr. Carl S. Dentzel, Director, The Southwest Museum, Highland Park, Los Angeles, California; Lawrence Dinnean, Curator of Pictorial Collections, Suzanne H. Gallup, Reference Librarian, William Roberts, Reference Librarian, The Bancroft Library, Berkeley; Donald Dresden, Washington, D.C.; Frank Eaton, Nancy E. Ferguson, Eatons' Ranch, Wolf, Wyoming; James Ebert, Site Supervisor, Theodore Roosevelt Birthplace National Historic Site, New York, New York; Mary Fearey, New Braunfels, Texas; Arthur M. Fitts III, Assistant to the Executive Vice President, American Numismatic Association, Colorado Springs, Colorado; Eleanor M. Gehres, Head, Augustino Mastroguiseppe, Curator of Photographs, Western History Collection, Denver Public Library, Denver; Ellen Glover, Research Assistant, Paula West, Assistant Photographer, Wyoming State Archives, Historical and Museum Department, Cheyenne; Michael Hooks, Deputy Archivist, David Murrah, University Archivist, The Southwest Collection, Texas Tech University, Lubbock; Judith Kremsdorf Golden, Photograph Librarian, Colorado Historical Society, Denver; Gene M. Gressley, Director, David Crosson, Research Historian, Annabelle McNamee, Senior Clerk, Western History Research Center, University of Wyoming, Laramie; Frances M. Gupton, Registrar, Amon Carter Museum of Western Art, Fort Worth, Texas; Archibald Hanna, Curator of Western Americana, Beinecke Rare Book and Manuscript Library, Yale University, New Haven, Connecticut; Melancthon W. Jacobus, Curator of Prints, Connecticut Historical Society, Hartford; Alan Jutzi, Assistant Curator of Rare Books, Daniel H. Woodward, Librarian, The Huntington Library, Art Gallery and Botanical Gardens, San Marino, California; Claire Kuehn, Archivist, Byron Price, Curator of History, Panhandle-Plains Historical Museum, Canyon, Texas; Roby Kuhn, Los Banos, California; Don Kunitz, Head, Sherry Smith, Bibliographic Assistant, Special Collections, University of California, Davis; Garry Kurutz, Library Director, Laverne Dicker, Photographs Curator, Lynn Donovan, Manuscript Librarian, Catherine Hoover, Exhibits Curator, Maude K. Swingle, Reference Librarian, California Historical Society, San Francisco; William Leingang, Curator, Norman Paulson, Curator, Frank Vyzralek, Archivist, State Historical Society of North Dakota, Bismarck; Irene Lichens, Librarian, Society of California Pioneers, San Francisco; Robert W. Lovett, Curator of Manuscripts and Archives, Baker Library, Harvard University, Boston; Shirley Markley, Administrator, National Trust for Historic Preservation, Washington, D.C.; Glenn Mason, Director, Lane County Pioneer Museum, Eugene, Oregon; Harriet Meloy, Librarian, Lory Morrow, Photo Archivist, Rex Myers, Research Librarian, Montana Historical Society, Helena; Michael Menard, Archivist, Historical Museum and Institute of Western Colorado, Grand Junction; Dr. Ernest Mittelberger, Director, San Francisco Wine Museum, San Francisco; Robert Monroe, Head, Dennis Andersen, Assistant, Sandra Kroupa, Assistant, Special Collections, Suzzalo Library, Seattle, Washington; Howard A. Nelson, De Kalb, Illinois; Edward Nolan, Archivist, Seattle Historical Society, Seattle, Washington; Bernice Otasue, National Wool Growers Association, Washington, D.C.; Minerva King Patch, Corpus Christi, Texas; Frances C. Petterson, Museum Director, Union Pacific Historical Museum, Omaha, Nebraska; Mary Alice Pettis, Bonham, Texas; Kenneth Pettitt, Supervising Librarian, Thomas Fante, Librarian, California State Library, Sacramento; Felix Revello, Supervisor, De Morès Historic Site, Medora, North Dakota; Karen Rubie, Vice President, Jefferson County Genealogical Society, Fairfield, Iowa; Martin Schmitt, Librarian, Carrie Singleton, Assistant, Special Collections, University of Oregon Library, Eugene; Kelli Shaw, Research Assistant, Western History Collection, University of Oklahoma, Norman; Lelon G. Shelton, Supervising Ranger, Bidwell Mansion State Historic Park, Chico, California; Nancy Sherbert, Photo and Map Curator, Kansas State Historical Society, Topeka; Frederic Snowden, Registrar, De Young Memorial Museum, San Francisco, California; Cecilia Steinfeldt, Curator of Decorative Arts, Witte Memorial Museum, San Antonio, Texas; Tatiana Tontarski, Technical Information Specialist, National Agricultural Library, Beltsville, Maryland; John M. Townley, Director, Phillip Earl, Curator of Exhibits, Nevada Historical Society, Reno; Clyde F. Trudell, Sausalito, California; Mavis Williams, President, Ellwood House Museum, De Kalb, Illinois; Janice Worden, Photographs Librarian, Oregon Historical Society, Portland; Karen Zoltenko, Archival Research, Division of State Archives and Public Records, Denver, Colorado.

BIBLIOGRAPHY

Abbott, E. C., and Helena Huntington Smith, *We Pointed Them North.* University of Oklahoma Press, 1955.

Albright, John, "Historic Resource Study and Historic Structure Report, Historical Data, Grant-Kohrs National Historic Site, Montana" (unpublished manuscript).

Angel, Myron, ed., *History of Nevada, 1881.* Hal Norton Books, 1958.

Athearn, Robert G., *Westward The Briton.* University of Nebraska Press, 1953.

Atherton, Lewis, *The Cattle Kings.* University of Nebraska Press, 1972.

Austin, Mary, *The Flock.* William Gannon, 1906 (Reprint 1973).

Beck, Warren A., *New Mexico.* University of Oklahoma Press, 1962.

Bidwell, John, *Echoes of the Past.* Arno Press, 1973 (Reprint).

Billington, Ray Allen, *Westward Expansion.* The Macmillan Company, 1967.

Bonsal, Stephen, *Edward Fitzgerald Beale.* G. P. Putnam's Sons, 1912.

Brisbin, James S., *The Beef Bonanza; or, How to Get Rich on the Plains.* University of Oklahoma Press, 1959 (Reprint).

Brown, Mark, *The Plainsmen of the Yellowstone.* University of Nebraska Press, 1961.

Brown, Mark, and W. R. Felton, *Before Barbed Wire.* Bramhall House, 1956.

Bullock, H. D., ed., *Decatur House.* National Trust for Historic Preservation, 1967.

Butcher, Solomon D., *Pioneer History of Custer County, Nebraska.* Sage Books, 1965.

Call, Mrs. Hughie, *Golden Fleece.* Houghton, 1942.

Carosso, Vincent P., *The California Wine Industry.* University of California Press, 1951.

Clay, John, *My Life on the Range.* University of Oklahoma Press, 1962.

Cleland, Robert Glass, *The Cattle on a Thousand Hills.* The Huntington Library, 1941.

Conard, Howard Louis, *Uncle Dick Wootton,* Milo Milton Quaife, editor. The Lakeside Press, 1957.

Connor, Seymour V., *Texas.* Thomas Y. Crowell Company, Inc., 1971.

Curry, Larry, ed., *The American West.* Viking Press, 1972.

Denhardt, Robert Moorman, *The King Ranch Quarter Horses.* University of Oklahoma Press, 1970.

Dick, Everett, *Conquering the Great American Desert.* Nebraska State Historical Society, 1975.

Dobie, J. Frank, *The Mustangs.* Little, Brown and Company, 1952.

Douglass, William A., and Jon Bilbao, *Amerikanuak*. University of Nevada Press, 1975.

Drago, Harry Sinclair, *Great American Cattle Trails*. Bramhall House, 1965.

Dresden, Donald, *The Marquis de Morès*. University of Oklahoma Press, 1970.

Ferris, Robert G., ed., *Prospector, Cowhand, and Sodbuster*. U.S. Department of the Interior, 1967.

Fletcher, Robert H., *Free Grass to Fences*. University Publishers Incorporated, 1960.

Forrest, Earle R., *Arizona's Dark and Bloody Ground*. Caxton Printers, 1936.

Frink, Maurice, *Cow Country Cavalcade*. The Old West Publishing Company, 1954.

Frink, Maurice, W. Turrentine Jackson and Agnes Wright Spring, *When Grass Was King*. University of Colorado Press, 1956.

Gage, Jack, *Tensleep and No Rest*. Prairie Publishing Company, 1958.

Gates, Paul W.: *California Ranchos and Farms*. The State Historical Society of Wisconsin, 1967.
The Farmer's Age. Harper & Row, Publishers, 1960.

Gilfillan, Archer B., *Sheep*. Little, Brown and Company, 1930.

Gressley, Gene M., *Bankers and Cattlemen*. University of Nebraska Press, 1966.

Grover, David H., *Diamondfield Jack*. University of Nevada Press, 1968.

Hagedorn, Hermann, *Roosevelt in the Bad Lands*. Houghton Mifflin Company, 1921.

Historical and Biographical Record of The Cattle Industry of Texas and Adjacent Territories, Vols. I and II. Antiquarian Press, Ltd., 1959.

Hunt, Rockwell D., *John Bidwell*. Caxton Printers, Ltd., 1942.

Kennedy, Michael S., ed., *Cowboys and Cattlemen*. Hastings House, Publishers, 1964.

Kupper, Winifred, *The Golden Hoof*. Alfred A. Knopf, Inc., 1945.

Lavender, David, *California*. W. W. Norton & Company, Inc., 1976.

Laxalt, Robert, "Basque Sheepherders," *National Geographic*, Vol. 129, No. 6. June 1966.

Lea, Tom, *The King Ranch*. Little, Brown and Company, 1957.

Lehmann, V. W., *Forgotten Legions*. Texas Western Press, 1969.

Leonard, Willard, "A Boyhood with Sheep in the Oregon Desert," *Oregon Historical Quarterly*, Vol. 76, No. 4. December 1975.

McCallum, Henry D. and Frances T., *The Wire that Fenced the West*. University of Oklahoma Press, 1965.

McWilliams, Carey: *Factories in the Field*. Peregrine Publishers, Inc., 1971.
Southern California Country. Duell, Sloan & Pearce, 1946.

Malone, Michael P., and Richard B. Roeder, *Montana*. University of Washington Press, 1976.

Mathers, Michael, *Sheepherders, Men Alone*. Houghton Mifflin Company, 1975.

Mattes, Merrill J., *The Great Platte River Road*. Nebraska State Historical Society Publications, Vol. XXV, 1969.

Maudslay, Robert *Texas Sheepman*, Winifred Kupper, editor. Books for Libraries Press, 1971 (Reprint).

Miller, Henry, "Management of Miller & Lux Ranches" (unpublished manuscript).

Mokler, Alfred James, *History of Natrona County, Wyoming*. Chicago Lakeside Press, 1923.

Nordhoff, Charles, *California: For Health, Pleasure and Residence,* 1873.

Nordyke, Lewis, *Great Roundup*. William Morrow & Company, 1955.

Osgood, Ernest Staples, *The Day of the Cattleman*. The University of Chicago Press, 1929.

Patterson, Edna B., Louise A. Ulph and Victor Goodwin, *Nevada's Northeast Frontier*. Western Printing and Publishing Company, 1969.

Putnam, Carleton, *Theodore Roosevelt,* Vol. I. Charles Scribner's Sons, 1958.

Roosevelt, Theodore: *The Autobiography of Theodore Roosevelt,* Wayne Andrews, editor. Octagon Books, 1975 (Reprint).
Ranch Life in the Far West. Northland Press, 1968 (Reprint).

Sandoz, Mari, *The Cattlemen*. Hastings House, Publishers, 1975 (Reprint).

Sewall, William Wingate, *Bill Sewall's Story of T. R.* Harper and Brothers, 1919.

"The Shepherds of Colorado," *Harper's New Monthly Magazine,* January 1880.

Smith, Sarah, *Adobe Days*. Primavera Press, 1931.

Sprague, Marshall, *A Gallery of Dudes*. Little, Brown and Company, 1967.

Starr, Kevin, *Americans and the California Dream*. Oxford University Press, 1973.

Stevenson, Richard W., ed., *The Land Ownership Atlas*. U.S. Government Printing Office, 1967.

Stevenson, Robert Louis, *Napa Wine*. John Henry Nash, 1924.

Stewart, George R., *Good Lives*. Houghton Mifflin Company, 1967.

Stuart, Granville, *Forty Years on the Frontier as Seen in the Journals and Reminiscences of Granville Stuart,* Paul C. Phillips, editor. The Arthur H. Clark Company, 1967.

Taper, Bernard, "The King of Ranchers," *American Heritage,* Vol. 18, No. 5. August 1967.

Towne, Charles Wayland, and Edward Norris Wentworth: *Cattle & Men*. University of Oklahoma Press, 1955.
Shepherd's Empire. University of Oklahoma Press, 1945.

Treadwell, Edward F., *The Cattle King*. Valley Publishers, 1950.

Treece, Paul Robert, "Mr. Montana: The Life of Granville Stuart, 1834-1918," (unpublished doctoral dissertation, Ohio State University, 1974).

Tweton, D. Jerome, *The Marquis de Morès*. North Dakota Institute for Regional Studies, 1972.

Webb, Walter Prescott, *The Great Plains*. Blaisdell Publishing Company, 1959.

Webb, Walter Prescott, and Carroll Bailey, eds., *The Handbook of Texas,* Vols. I and II. The Texas State Historical Association, 1952.

Wellman, Paul I., *The Trampling Herd*. Cooper Square Publishers, Inc., 1974.

Wentworth, Edward Norris, *America's Sheep Trails*. Iowa State College Press, 1948.

Woody, Clara T., and Milton L. Schwartz, *Globe, Arizona*. Arizona Historical Society, 1977.

Wyman, Walker D., *The Wild Horse of the West*. University of Nebraska Press, 1963 (Reprint).

Yost, Nellie Snyder, *The Call of the Range*. Sage Books, 1966.